HOW TO START A MOBILE

DJ Business

How To Start A Mobile DJ Business

ISBN: 979-8-218-63408-7

Library of Congress Number: 2025906773

HOW TO START A MOBILE

DJ Business

A complete guide to help you go
from being a DJ Hobbyist to a DJ Hero

René Velazquez

To the Love of my life, Josie,

You are the beautiful song guiding my heart. Every day with you celebrates the love we share and the beautiful story we are creating together. Let's keep the music playing.

Contents

Introduction

I dedicate this book to my father, his father (my grandfather) and to my family who continue to live within the gift of music. My grandfather was a DJ in the early 1970s. He would delight the crowds at a place named "Close Encounters", near 47th and Racine, on Chicago's southside. As a very young child, I remember walking into this "disco" and seeing music, lights, crowds, and watching disco dancing for the first time. My father started DJing a bit later in the 1970s and continued to carry on the "family DJ legacy" for over 40 years. When my father started, I remember he and my mother hosting parties for the entire block we lived on (28th street in Bridgeport, Chicago). My father would turn his speakers toward the front windows and soon after, we would have a big crowd of people dancing in the streets, walking in and out of our tiny little apartment. My sisters and I would try to sleep, sharing our bed space with piles of leather coats. I also remember peeking out of my bedroom and watching Police officers standing around enjoying themselves at these street parties. It was a different time back then!

My DJ career began in the late 1980s during the Chicago House Music explosion, the evolution of "Freestyle", the birth of "Grunge", and the beginning of the Hip Hop generation. What a time to be alive! When I wasn't breakdancing on the streets with my friends, I was learning how to mix vinyl records on my father's belt drive turntables. I wasn't always allowed to use his equipment, so I would sneak my DJ practice when both of my parents weren't home.

Growing up, I would help my father with his DJ gigs. Between helping set up and take down his DJ gear, I was one of the lucky few who was able to watch my father work his magic. My father really knew how to control the crowds, and he did it without mixing, scratching, or doing any type of DJ tricks. He knew what his crowds wanted, and he gave it to them, every time. Later, he teamed up with his cousin, Tony, and created a dynamic duo of DJs. My father and "Uncle Tony" (R.I.P.) created some of Chicago's hottest parties and special events. At my father's funeral, people were still talking about the pure joy he would bring to their events and to so many other people who heard him play.

R.I.P. Dad, August 2021.

It wasn't until the 1990s that I began to DJ like my father (and his father) did. I purchased my own equipment and started DJing my own parties. However, instead of vinyl, my father suggested that I start working with CDs. So, I took what I learned from him over the years and put the process into action! My father and I would sometimes bond over our gigs, talk about new music, share fun stories. As my skills progressed and showed that I was able to handle real parties, he would give me the DJ gigs he couldn't (or didn't want to) do. When I needed special music, he always "burned" it onto a CD for me. I was proud to continue my father and grandfather's legacy.

This book is also dedicated to my cousins, Marty, Hector, and Andres (Chicago's own DJ Smiley). We grew up together and took our DJ hobby out of our homes and into the dance factories, gymnasiums, banquet halls, and nightclubs all over the Chicago area. Let's not forget my oldest son, Michael, who DJ'd in college and his daughter (my granddaughter) Delilah, who has showed me sparks of interest in DJing herself one day! Our love for music transcends over anything else. Because of my father, we will always have music to bring us together. Another special mention... my kids. I used to wake my kids up at 2, 3, 4 in the morning after my gigs because I needed help carrying my equipment back into the house. I know they hated doing it, but they were the beneficiaries of the money I made. Thanks, kids! I love you.

From vinyl, cassette tapes, CDs, USBs and external drives... I have been in the DJ industry for a long time and have lived through some major evolutions of music. I have a personal story unlike other DJs, but the concept is the same. I hope to translate this concept into something special for you, no matter your background, age, or style of music. I will be unleashing my DJ secrets and experiences here so anyone with the desire to move people with music can do it without fear. I also want you to have an amazing time doing it. I hope to help take your DJ hobby to an honorable lifestyle so you can put yourself in a position to start your own successful mobile DJ business.

Enjoy!

Chapter 1

Becoming A DJ

Who Is This Book For?

This book is for those who've imagined standing behind the decks of a DJ booth with the music flowing through your fingertips, and the crowd moving in perfect rhythm with your beats. Whether you're playing new tracks in your bedroom, playing at house parties for your friends, or envisioning yourself on festival stage in front of hundreds of people, you may already have a DJs most important ingredient – The desire to create and share music. It takes months, even years, to learn the DJ skills necessary to start a business. But, playing music, watching people dance and enjoying themselves to music you play is a feeling like no other. Music transcends communication because music can move people without words. DJing is more than just a hobby– it's an art form, a musical journey, and for many, DJing is a life-changing career.

However, learning to DJ is like learning a new language. You will need to learn the terms, the techniques, and you'll need to stay current with new technology just to communicate with your peers and to stay relevant. Just remember: A motion picture with the newest and most amazing special effects doesn't always make the best movie, a photographer with the highest resolution camera doesn't always take the best pictures, and a Chef with high-tech cooking utensils doesn't always prepare the best meal. A true DJ will learn how to build the vibe of any event, master the skill of reading their crowds, and create lasting, memorable events for their clients; something today's technological advances may never learn how to do.

"You don't choose the DJ business; the DJ business chooses you."

Every successful DJ started somewhere. Every single one of them started not knowing how to turn on the equipment or press the right button at the right time. But here's the secret: Every DJ started with a dream, a love for music, and a fire deep inside themselves to make it happen. DJing isn't just about playing music. It's about creating unforgettable moments, igniting emotions, and taking people on a musical journey you create. The energy and the connection to the crowd is undeniable. It all starts with your music. You need to be able to take your music and share it with the masses. You must step into the arena and perform before you figure out what moves you or what direction you will want your DJ career to go. At the beginning of your DJ journey, don't worry about "picking a niche". Not yet. You need to feel the true energy of a dance floor, and you need to learn how to keep the party going before you make any type of decision on any niche. Period. There is no manual in the world that will teach you how to do that. The crowds and the people you encounter along the way will decide which direction your DJ career will go. The first time you get behind the DJ table and take the party/event to its highest levels... you will never forget it. It's the moment you never look back. The euphoria that comes from a packed dance floor and making the crowd scream when you play their favorite songs is unforgettable. The most legendary DJs in the business have mastered this skill. You can, too!

Think about this for a moment: Any DJ is about 85% of any party or celebration. So, it's no secret why the DJ industry attracts more and more aspiring DJs every year. Once a person masters the technical skills of being a DJ, that person also needs to hone their creative instincts into business strategies to transform their skills into a fruitful business. You must be able to do more than just deliver electrifying sets; you also need to create a DJ brand that attracts paying clients. It's an industry filled with opportunity!

In order to become a great DJ, there may be a few things in your life that will have to change. For instance, you will be spending a lot of late nights out, your weekends and Holidays may be replaced by spending time with strangers, and the perks of having sick time and paid vacation days on the job are over. If you are a person who needs to take breaks when you feel tired, the DJ life probably isn't for you... and that's ok because being a DJ isn't for everyone. Being a committed DJ also means you must maintain professionalism, you must control your alcohol consumption, and your emotional intelligence must be at its highest levels. One more thing: Have you ever considered how DJ equipment gets to and from every location? That is *your* job. DJ equipment can become very heavy, especially when you are exhausted. If you are ok with these points, you may have what it takes to adjust into the DJ lifestyle. In that case, welcome to the DJ life!

What To Expect

To become a great DJ, you will need to expect, then adapt to a few things. If you are not very good at taking criticism, you will never make it. The best DJs can take criticism and use that advice to build better skills. Expect the audience (usually made up mostly of perfect strangers) to give you criticism, good and bad, regarding your DJ skills. Most times, you'll get a complaint about a certain song being played. No problem, that should be easy to handle. Other times, you'll get the people who give real feedback on your DJ set, and it can sometimes change your game, making you better. However, the real test of your DJ character is when you get feedback from the alcohol-induced guests who are not very nice. A good way to handle these special critics is to remember this great quote: *"Do not be distracted by criticism. Remember – the only taste of success some people get is to take a bite out of you."* - Zig Ziglar.

Another expectation in the DJ industry is an ever-changing, ever-evolving music scene, no matter the genre you decide to work in. A good DJ keeps up with changing times and keeps their music library fresh. No matter how robust you think your music library is, you will need to keep your library current and up to date because new music and new artists are always emerging. This is a bigger challenge than you may think. We will go a little deeper into this subject in a later Chapter. Expect to stay current with music you don't like (and sometimes hate) because your clients will want to hear it. A perfect example is the song, "Celebration" – Kool and the Gang. I played it so much I started to hate it. I hated it so much I never brought it to my events. After a guest had asked for it, and I didn't play it, the event organizer mentioned it to me after the event. Ever since that day, I made it a point to keep it in my library. So, no matter how much you don't like a song, remember that your job is to play it.

Lastly, expect a family-like support system. I have met DJs from all over the country and every single one was a part of an amazing DJ network. DJs are cool people on so many levels. Many of the DJs you will meet on your journey will become your friends, mentors, and sometimes new family members, so treat them as such. If you learn and respect the unwritten DJ "codes", you will be welcomed with open arms. You should always <u>show up to gigs early</u>, never steal the set of a fellow DJ, never play your sets "in the red" (especially if DJs are scheduled to work after you), give space to the DJ on the decks, help keep the DJ booth clear of unwanted outsiders, never undercut another fellow DJ on price to steal a gig, etc., etc. If you just stay respectful, use common sense, and do great work, you will never have a problem. The DJ community is small but thriving and very strong. Find the best DJ community to engage with and grow with them.

Basic DJ Skills

DJing isn't just about pressing play. It's about commanding a crowd and telling a beautiful story with sound. And that story begins with the DJs connection to their music. It's spiritual. DJs just don't hear a song, they dissect it. They understand the song's bassline, they feel the emotional rise and fall of the melodies, and they capture the moods of every bar. No matter what type of music you love, your music library is where your DJ career begins. The best DJs have plenty of music to share with their audiences. It's like having a conversation without words, so you'll need a healthy music library to communicate!

To get started on your mobile DJ journey, your basic equipment (or gear) should be simple and inexpensive. The most important piece of equipment is going to be your laptop. The laptop is the heart and soul of your setup, so I suggest you use a laptop with up-to-date specifications of today. Loaded onto your laptop will be the DJ software to play and manipulate the songs in your music library. If you are just getting started, I suggest you load the free software available. If you are at the very beginning of a DJ career, this is all you need to start. If you are a little more advanced, you will want to have a controller (or mixer) so you can physically manipulate the songs by setting up cues, scratching, applying special effects, etc. to really get into it. If you have a controller, you'll need speakers to bring your practice sets to life! Either way, you must have a DJ setup of some kind to get it going. As I was growing up, I would use my father's belt-driven turntables and a 2-channel mixer, but it worked. Later, I was able to work with a DJ component that had 2 CD players, and a mixer built into one unit. I loved it because it was so convenient and easy to set up wherever I played. When I wasn't DJing, I was able to hang out with other DJs who were much more advanced than I was. I was fortunate because they would give me advice and tips on mixing songs. So, the most essential element of learning to DJ is practicing, no matter what types of equipment you have. Practice is key!

To become one of the great DJs in your area, you will need to learn a few skills before you decide to orchestrate parties and events on your own. In today's world, people are *expecting* DJs to have basic skills before they stand behind the DJ booth. Save yourself enormous amounts of time, money, effort, and complete embarrassment by learning these basic skills first! Whether you plan to work with turntables or controllers or both, you must become familiar (and very comfortable) with executing and understanding the following terms:

- Mixing/Beatmatching/Sync
- Breaks/Phrasing/Cutting
- Blending/Transitions/Pitch
- EQs
- Stems
- Looping
- Cues
- Scratching

As you get more and more acquainted with your equipment, you will become more comfortable with learning tricks and techniques that work for you. However, it will never happen overnight. DJing takes months, even years, to learn and master. One of the best ways to learn how to DJ is to record yourself. Set up your phone or camera nearby and record your sets. Replay your sets later and listen very carefully to your transitions. Ask yourself questions like: Am I playing the right songs? Are they being matched correctly? Is the vibe right? Are the cues in the right places? Are the songs mixing at the perfect break (or phrase)? For a real assessment of your skills, ask someone else to listen to your recording and get their feedback. Trust me, the looks on their faces never lie.

Another idea is to hook up your equipment to your phone and stream your sessions onto social media for feedback. Your fans or followers may catch something you may have missed. Also, create video clips. Post longer video clips onto YouTube (where longer clips are acceptable). Post the smaller clips onto other social media platforms where short clips are the norm. Many DJs today like to post a clip of a transition of 1, 2, or 3 songs. This is such a great way to get your name (and your brand) out there because your future clients will be able to watch you create your magic!

Side note: In my 20+ years of DJing events, I have never needed to scratch the music in my sets. So, I never learned how to do it very well. If you feel a need to scratch and do tricks on your set, do your thing and be the best. Just keep in mind that too much scratching may kill the dance floor, depending on the audience. My suggestion is to scratch occasionally, just to add a little spice to your set, not much more. The dance floor will appreciate it.

Chapter 2

Your 1ˢᵗ Gigs

How To Get Your 1ˢᵗ Gig

Your first goal to having a DJ business should be to take your hobby of playing music for yourself (and a small number of people) and do it for a real crowd. To get your first gig, you will need to have basic equipment, preferably equipment that can comfortably host a party for about 30 to 50 people. Make sure the equipment sounds great, even at high volume levels. You will also need to have mastered (or be very familiar with) the basic DJ skills mentioned earlier because you'll need your confidence in a good place!

Next step is to talk to your immediate contacts (friends, family, co-workers) about DJing their next gig. Offer to provide music for the next BBQ, company event, pool party, Holiday celebration, etc. If they offer to pay you, excellent. However, don't expect to get paid for your first gig. As an aspiring DJ, you should probably offer to do your first gigs for free. Trust me, the experience you will get from these gigs is worth 100X more than any dollar amount you will ever get paid.

Tip: Make more connections with other DJs. Most DJs in the business look out for each other, so most of them will likely welcome anyone who wants to become a great DJ like themselves. You can find DJs at company picnics, networking events, car shows, coffee shops, BBQs, tailgating parties, etc. I've also seen DJs at book signings, car wash fundraisers, corporate presentations, and shopping malls. The list is endless. Approach the DJ and make them your buddy!

Another way to get started would be to "shadow" a DJ for a larger DJ company. Become an assistant to an established DJ and learn the business by helping that DJ work events. If you can shadow a good DJ, you will have a golden opportunity to learn some valuable techniques in the business. Take the lessons you learn here and begin to structure your own methods. **Tip**: Always take photos and videos to document your experience. (You will definitely be needing these later!)

Public Permits. Check your local ordinances because you may need a permit to DJ in a public area. Purchase the permit to DJ on a busy street corner, at a busy park, near a river or lake where people congregate. My suggestion is to DJ during a lunch hour near a business district of some type. The workers will be attracted by the music and will gravitate toward you. It's also the best way for your potential clients to see you in action! It's important that you look great while you get the crowd moving, so dress like you mean business. This will greatly increase your chances of gaining new clients. Purchase a few permits and offer a regular "lunchtime mix" or an "After Work Wind-Down" to help people escape from their grueling office work. A small, but effective setup would work perfectly. If this idea works, you may want to consider creating a business card with a QR Code to pass out. Lead visitors to your website.

Small Business Partnerships. Business owners with storefronts are <u>always</u> looking for ways to increase traffic to their stores! Introduce yourself and work out a deal to play music to attract customers. Play for free promotion for your brand or play for a small cash fee. You should also offer to get on the mic to promote their business to passersby. I had a friend of mine ask me to set up my DJ equipment for the Grand Opening of his Tire Shop. We had a great time and I got paid a percentage of the sales that came in. This idea can work for just about any storefront or high-traffic area.

Charging For Your DJ Service

After your first successful gig or 2, you may want to start charging for your services. It takes effort to haul your equipment everywhere! Just make sure you get paid <u>before</u> the gig or at the start of the event. Having to "chase" the client for payment after services rendered is a big mistake. Get payment early or you will run the risk of never getting paid (or getting paid short). **Tip:** Keep all your financial transactions at a professional level by having something in writing. You can create an ultra-simple contract, or you can do something more elaborate. Either way, having something in writing will protect you and prevent the client from booking someone else. You are just starting out, so it's not critical that you have an official contract at this point, but it's nice to have.

After your first gigs, the guests at the event may ask for your business card. If you do not have one, politely get their contact information and follow up later. If you do not get asked for your business card, it might mean that you may not have done such a great job. It happens. Don't give up! If you are truly committed to learning the DJ business, you will want another chance to do it again. Perhaps the music was too loud, maybe the requests you played killed the party's "vibe", maybe you were on the mic too much, you may have created the wrong energy, or maybe you made too many simple mistakes. These are easy fixes. If the client who paid you is not happy with your service, you may want to talk about what happened. Make the proper adjustments to your set, then offer to DJ their next party for no charge to win back their confidence. This is a very humbling experience to go through, but it works in getting those next gigs!

Building Your Music Library

One of the biggest differences between the "old school" DJs and the DJs of today is buying music. I feel the DJs of today are being robbed of the experience of walking into a real DJ record store. Back when record stores were the place to buy music, DJs had to know where to go to get the hottest tracks of the day. There were larger, more "corporate" stores like Rose Records (where my father used to take me), but then there were the smaller, "boutique-type" record stores that sold the hot club music all the DJs were looking for. In Chicago, my favorites were: Hot Jamz, Loop Records, Imports, and Let's Boogie on 33rd & Halsted (R.I.P. Neal). As soon as you walked in, you would hear (and feel) the music pounding, you would see real DJs cashing customers out at the register, and the smell of vinyl records filled the air. It was an unforgettable experience! It always gave me a rush to see the hottest DJs in the city looking in the same record section as you. At times, you would be able to strike up a quick conversation and end up finding out about the best parties in the city! It was also a fun time to eavesdrop and hear other DJs tell their stories of the crazy Chicago nightlife. Other times, you might catch a music celebrity (or new artist) trying to promote the newest single to the customers. What a rush! These were the days when DJs had to buy an extra copy of a record in order to do the tricks and "special effects" for the crowds. The controllers and mixers of today have buttons to do that now. Do you know why DJs today like to lift their hands up, and dance for the crowd, and seem to have time to "showboat" on stage? It's because they don't have to look for records in record crates! Back in the day, DJs would have to look for records in record crates, usually in dark places or poorly lit DJ booths to find the next songs to play. The DJ needed to know exactly where the songs were and needed to be super quick to get those records on the decks.

Building a solid music library is one of the biggest keys to your success. Popular songs are easy to find, but it's just as important to have new music in your playlists, too. Here are some key places to buy new music today:

- Record pools
- Record clubs
- Streaming platforms
- Concert merchandise booths
- Directly from music artists
- Record collectors

Whether you join a record pool/club, buy from music stores, from a specialty record collector, you will need to have only high-quality music files in your library. I suggest you buy only high-quality files because these files tend to maintain their sound integrity and are easily copied and transferred with little to no issues. Never steal music from websites like YouTube because the quality is terrible, no matter how much you edit.

As you purchase more popular music, please keep in mind that some of the songs may have explicit lyrics. What I would usually do when purchasing music is buy both the clean version and the explicit version of each song. I would play the clean versions at Weddings and more corporate-like events, and I would play the same song (the explicit versions) when it is more acceptable like at a bar, lounge, or nightclub. Record pools tend to have multiple versions of songs like remixes and EDM versions, so take a listen before you buy because sometimes the remix can be overdone. Personally, I like to buy the original songs because I like to see the crowd sing to the songs I play. Sometimes when you play a song that has been "over produced," it becomes unrecognizable, and crowds don't respond to it as much. Lastly, always keep your songs in folders properly labeled in your drives. If you do this in the early DJ stages, it will help you tremendously when you really need it!

Keeping your music library clean and organized is critical to success for 2 main reasons. The first reason is to save you from paying for the same song multiple times. When you have thousands and thousands of songs in your library, buying the same music repeatedly can become very costly. The other reason is to be able to retrieve your music in the fastest times possible. During events, a good DJ knows what to play 3 or 4 songs ahead of time. However, as you are preparing the next songs, you may see the crowd energy shift. That usually means that you should shift the songs you had planned and change the next song to elevate the crowd. Or, if you see the crowd isn't vibing, you may want to take the crowd in a different direction. Either way, you will need to know *exactly* where your next song is to be able to switch it up on a moment's notice! The efficiency of your music library is another key to having smooth DJ sets.

"The more you love music, the more music you love." - **Billy Crystal**

Staying current with new songs is tricky. It is not as easy as looking at the music charts or doing an online search for new music. Just think about the Top 20 songs that were played on the radio last year at this time. Are they still being played? Are they considered "classics"? Chances are that these songs are probably long gone and forgotten. So, it's important to sharpen your senses to recognize good music. You will need to always keep your eyes and ears open. **Tip:** Just because a song is new, doesn't always mean it's a good song. And just because the hottest artist puts out a new song, doesn't mean it should go into your library! While travelling in your car, switch to different radio stations to see which songs get heavy play. For "dinner music", listen to the soft rock stations and find some good ones there. For the newer music, listen to the pop music stations where you can usually hear a "top songs of the week" list. Pay close attention to the songs that "crossover" to other radio stations because those are the songs that have a much greater appeal to bigger audiences. Those songs are usually the songs you "must have" in your library. Also pay attention to the artists performing (and winning) on music award shows, Super Bowl halftime shows and pay attention to large corporations who sponsor music artists. Along with that, pay attention to the songs other DJs play in their sets that really move their crowds. These are the songs you must have in your music files, too. Local artists are usually a good source of music, but not all of them. As long as you're paying close attention to the music scene, you'll always be ready for your next gigs. Clients always appreciate the DJ who knows what's happening in music!

Making Mistakes

"One who makes a mistake and does nothing to correct it, has already made a second mistake." - **Unknown**

Really knowing your music is critical to your success. At the beginning of your career, you will never have a perfect set and that's ok. Remember that you are just getting started. You're not a polished professional… yet. You are going to make mistakes, and some will be bigger than others. You will miss transitions, you will drop equipment, you will kill a dance floor, you will say something wrong on the mic, you will get nervous, you will play the wrong song, so on and so on. Just remember that these are the things that will only make you better! No one is perfect, not even <u>you</u>. We usually see images of DJs doing a flawless job on the decks, but you rarely ever see a DJ making mistakes during a set. That's because they've already made their mistakes and have made the necessary corrections!

Here's a funny story: I was DJing a Holiday event for a new client. During dinner, I noticed that the Latinos in the crowd were really enjoying the music. So, I decided to give them a little "treat" and play a song that is popular within the Mexican culture. I'm Mexican, however, I don't know the Spanish language very well. I just knew this Spanish song was a Mexican crowd favorite. The song I played was "Las Mañanitas" by Trio del Los Panchos. In the middle of the song, a party guest came up to me and asked, "Who's birthday is it?" I was confused, so I just shrugged my shoulders and smiled. I later found out that the song I played is the Mexican birthday song! OMG. I played a Mexican birthday song at a Holiday party, and it wasn't anyone's birthday... How embarrassing! Needless to say, I've never made that mistake again. My advice to you is not to worry so much about making small mistakes. In fact, it's best to make the small mistakes as you begin your DJ journey, learn from them, and move on. This way, you won't make the bigger mistakes later!

Chapter 3

Crafting Your Brand

The Basics of Branding

Branding is how people perceive you when you're not there. As you begin your DJ career, you will start to build your brand by representing your style and your musical presentation to others. You will also begin to put more emphasis on things like the way you dress, the music you play, your setup, your interaction with the event planners, etc. You will begin to settle into your DJ "comfort zone". More people will notice your style, your music, and they'll begin to connect with both. These are your people! They're the ones who will have no problem picking up the phone and calling you for every event they have.

Back in the 1990s, the best branding for DJs was to get your name on a flyer or poster for a local dance party. I would watch my friends mix at parties for hours, for free, just for the opportunity to have their name on a flyer. But, just having their name on a flyer put them in the limelight. One of the other ways to brand yourself back then was to create cassette mixtapes (later it was CDs) and pass them out at parties or on the street.

Today, you can record your sets and post them online. Event promoters and organizers want to hear your sets, transitions, song choices, and watch your techniques before they hire you so it's important to have the videos, links, and streams ready. My suggestion to you is to try to think of different strategies that may work for yourself and your brand, then embrace it!

Establish your digital footprint. If you are doing great and are seriously considering owning a DJ company, now is the time to lock in a company name. I've never had an official DJ name, I just used the name of my father's old DJ company, "Good Times" (named after the song by Chic). Later, I used another company name to new capture audiences in the Wedding industry. When considering a name, choose one such as: (www.YourDJCompanyName.com), and make sure the name is available on the social media platforms you like. Get a unique name from a domain service that sells domains like GoDaddy.com, make sure there are no copyright or trademark laws protecting it, then lock it in. Do this before you start to apply for a business license because there is a good chance that the business name is available, but the social media name may not be. Next, create multiple social media accounts highlighting your new DJ career. Make these accounts business accounts. **Tip:** If you want a specific name and it is not available, consider putting the name of your city at the end of it like this: www.YourDJCompanyMYCITY.com. Don't forget to connect your "official" email address to your website. I cannot begin to tell you how many DJs in the field are using Gmail and Yahoo as their email address. High-paying clients don't take DJs very seriously if they are working with a generic email address. Get a real email address to get paid the real dollars. You'll need an email address because people who will be hiring you in the future will only want to communicate through email. The days of "hit me up" on my social or "DM me" are over. Real professionals work with real DJs through email because it's how they like to send contracts and get approvals to hire you!

Your 1st Website

If you want to take your services to the next level, you must create a website dedicated to your craft. **Tip:** There are plenty of website platforms for DJs, so just find the one that you're comfortable with. I used Wix.com for my websites because they were easy to build, and it allowed me to accept payments through the websites I made. For many DJs, a one-page website is all you might need. Once you get your website up, start to post your pictures, images, testimonials, and upcoming gigs for your future clients to see. Link your website to your social media accounts. To create a greater impact, have other friends and clients also link to your website and social media accounts.

Creating Your Logo

Once you have a name that fits perfectly for your new venture, you'll want to have a logo that makes a statement in the DJ industry. Here, you'll have 3 choices to make: You can hire someone to do it, you can create one yourself, or you can get help from Artificial Intelligence (A.I.). If you aren't very good with graphic design, I would suggest you hire a professional graphic designer. It can cost you a few dollars, but it saves you so much time and effort from doing it yourself. If you have some graphic design experience, make it yourself. Get creative. If you don't have the graphic design skills, but you want to save money (instead of paying a graphic designer), find a software program that helps create logos and also incorporates A.I. into its designs. My suggestion here is to be careful when using A.I. software because you're not the only person using the software to create a logo. **Tip:** Use these guidelines for creating a logo:

- Make sure your logo is appropriate for all audiences. Ensure that your logo is non-offensive to anyone. Especially keep your design away from religion, politics, and sex!

- Keep it simple. One of the ways to test a logo's simplicity is to be able to draw it in under 10 seconds. If you can't do this, your logo may be too complicated or too "noisy" for anyone to want to remember it.

- Your logo can always be changed later. You don't have to make it a permanent symbol.

- Let your branding/marketing do the work. Your logo is just a symbol of your company, it is <u>not</u> your brand.

- Finalize your logo into a vector format. (.eps, .ai, .svg, etc.) This will enable you to enlarge your logo to any size you want. You will need this in case you want to create a large banner, place it onto a billboard, or place it onto a DJ Booth someday in the future.

- Have different "versions" ready to go! Have a black one, a white one, a blue one, etc. because your clients or event organizers may need your logo on a flyer and you'll want your logo to stand out! Also, attorneys and doctors still use fax machines (for encryption purposes), so having an all-black version of your logo is good to send via fax.

- Make it stand out. You want your logo to stand out among other DJ logos or other DJ company logos.

Business Cards

Business cards are critical to your success. When creating your business cards, make a fantastic design. It is literally just a few dollars difference to go from a bad card to a great card. My advice here is to stay away from "cheap" and go full throttle on this. Your business card speaks to people when you are not there. It shows that you take yourself and your business seriously. A cheap card shows cheap services, and this is not how you want your business to be perceived, no matter how good you are. I have always had awesome looking business cards. Whenever I met people and introduced my business and my DJ services, my business card always left a lasting impression. **Tip:** A great looking business card will put your business on higher levels than other DJ companies trying to fly by with cheap cards and subpar designs.

An alternative to the traditional business card is to create an electronic business card. Once you have an awesome-looking business card made, it is important that you carry it everywhere you go. Always have it ready. You only have one chance to make a first impression, so having your business card presented at the right place and the right time can help you land some great gigs!

The Basics of Marketing

Marketing your DJ company is different from branding. Branding is your business identity; marketing helps you convert your sales and advertising efforts into paying clients. Posting flyers in bars, laundromats, libraries, car shows, etc. is one way to get the marketing going. On these flyers you should have your offer posted... 1/2 price on weekday gigs, $100 off your event, etc. When the flyer is created correctly in a digital format, you can also email (or direct message) these flyers to friends to easily share on social media. Posting consistently onto social media is great for marketing. I suggest posting regularly once or twice a week at least. Keep your message clear, make offers people want, and keep creating content consistently! The comments, likes, and shares to your posts can often turn into paying gigs!

Another marketing idea is to throw your own party. Have a bunch of partygoers come listen to you do your thing. During the gig, pass out your business cards and remind everyone that you are starting the hottest DJ company in the area. The goal is to book more gigs! Be clear about who to invite and make sure you do it in a well-known location (always looking out for your safety). Keep recording, keep taking photos, keep creating short videos, and keep posting live events. Doing this right (with good quality content) will help build your following quickly.

Consistently keep your eyes and ears open for more opportunities to DJ. Keep making connections because there is always an event happening soon. The chances of getting your next gig are always good. Ask just about anyone you know, right now, today, about an event coming up and they will tell you about a party or an event they know of coming soon. There is always a couple getting married, there is always a holiday coming, and there is always a birthday or anniversary celebration happening soon. **Tip:** Just because you find out an event has a DJ booked for the event, don't stop marketing. What if something happens and the DJ cannot make the event? Position yourself to potentially fill in for the DJ. Just let the event organizers that you'd love to be considered the DJ "backup" in case something happens. If you are available to fill in to cover the event, and you do a great job, you will look like an absolute hero!

Promote, promote, promote. When you visit an upscale restaurant, pass out your cards to the concierge, the Manager, or the servers. When you visit your bank, the bankers and the tellers may have an inside lead on an upcoming event. A local Chamber of Commerce is an organization that puts on events often so leave your business cards there. You get the idea. **Tip:** One of the ways I would gauge how well I did at events… I would count the number of business cards I gave away during and after the event. The more cards I gave away, the more calls I would usually get in return. I was always giving out business cards, so it meant that I always had a steady flow of business. It also meant that I was in control of my own schedule. I would turn down business whenever I needed some time off, and I would accept gigs when I needed the extra income. It was like running a faucet where I would control the drips and flows. When you get to this point, you are doing great. Continue practicing, keep networking, do a few more gigs, and soon you will be ready to elevate your DJ journey even further.

The most important thing to know about great marketing is to give your potential clients the very best service possible. This means responding to phone calls and emails immediately! You must remember that people who call you are looking for DJ services and may want to hire the first DJ company just to get the task off of their "things to do list". If you don't respond quickly, you run the risk of your competitor winning the business!

Chapter 4

Essential DJ Equipment

Your 1st Real Setup

Now that you have had a few gigs under your belt, it is time to start thinking about becoming a legitimate business and buying some real equipment. The equipment you have been using up to this point can now be considered your backup equipment. You're familiar with this gear, so you can always consider this as a quick setup. It will help calm your nerves if things were to ever go down! Some DJs prefer to rent new equipment, but I advise against it at the beginning. If you want to rent your gear (for write off purposes, for liability, storage logistics, etc.), I suggest you rent equipment on a regular basis to get familiar with the company, the equipment choices, and the rental return policies. For now, my suggestion is to buy your equipment.

When shopping for your new equipment, make sure it is what you need and not much more. I suggest you visit actual DJ stores or purchase "nearly new" equipment from private vendors. Now is the time to seriously consider what direction you would like your DJ career to go. If you plan on DJing more corporate, professional, or Wedding gigs, you will need to have equipment to deliver high quality music for venues that can hold about 500 people. If you are more comfortable DJing the smaller gigs like Grand Openings, school dances, outdoor events, etc., you may just need a set up to fill a room of about 250 people or less. Note: If you would rather DJ at nightclubs, you may not have to buy much equipment because the venue will provide it for you.

The main qualities of your new equipment should be based on are price, brand reliability, and durability. You will be packing and moving your equipment often, so I also suggest you purchase your equipment in black models because your equipment will, on occasion, hit walls, scrape doorways, and accidentally drop onto floors. Having black-colored equipment won't show the scratches and dents you will get along your DJ journey as much as with white-colored or silver-colored gear. One night, a Wedding guest kindly offered to help me take my equipment out to my car. It was a great Wedding, and I was exhausted, so I gladly accepted his nice gesture. Unbeknownst to me, the guest had quite a bit to drink. He was carrying my $1,500 speaker bumping and hitting everything in his path to my car. Ugh! It was the last time I ever let anyone help me carry my equipment!

Be careful during this stage of the game. Try to create a modest budget before you buy any equipment and stick to it because this is the time when you'll see the amazing DJ gear on the market. You'll be seeing the stuff high-end DJs are using and you'll want to have it. Do your best to resist! Stick to your budget and choose equipment with the lower price points. It's important to know what equipment is on the market, but don't get pulled into buying equipment that is too "advanced" for you. Remember, you need to master the basic skills before your career can take off. Consider buying your 1st DJ setup like buying your first car… make sure you know how to drive before you get the really nice car!

Basic DJ Setup

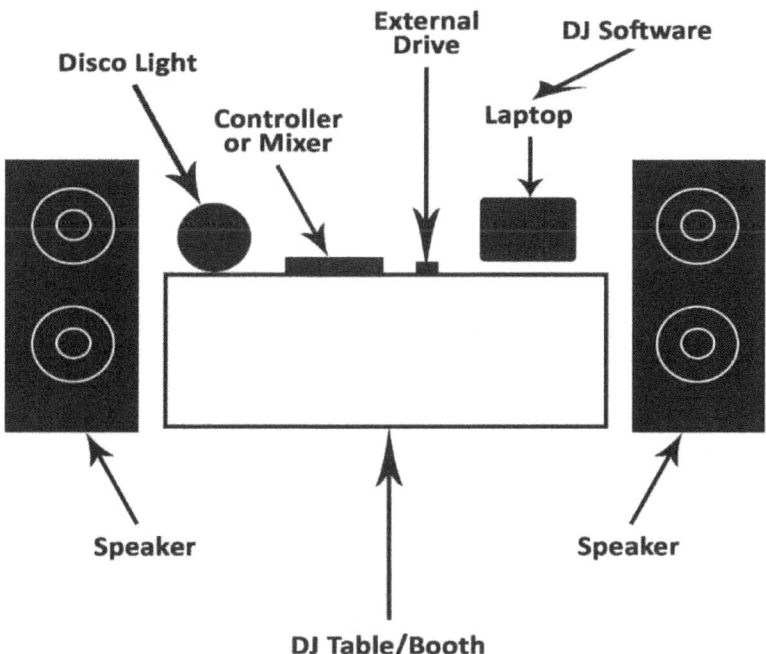

External Drive

DJ Software

Disco Light

Controller or Mixer

Laptop

Speaker

Speaker

DJ Table/Booth

The Basic Needs

For a basic professional mobile DJ setup, you will need:

- A reliable vehicle
- Good laptop (so you can keep up with software updates quickly and easily)
- DJ software
- Controller/Mixer (something easy to carry and set up)
- 4-foot Table (as a backup)
- External hard drive (a reliable place to you keep your music)
- Powered Speakers
- Microphone
- Disco Light/Lasers (a really good one, at the very least)
- Your "uniform"
- Backup equipment

The reliable vehicle. Do <u>not</u> underestimate the value of your car/van/truck. Your vehicle is an especially important part of your DJ equipment! For the readers who are not quite old enough to drive yet, think about the years of practice you can build upon before you get your Driver's License! I remember one Wedding event I was scheduled to DJ, and on the way there, my car began to overheat. Luckily, I left a half hour earlier than normal. I had to pull off to the side of the road and wait for the engine to cool before I continued to the event! (I made it on time. Whew!) After the gig, I stopped at a gas station to fill the car with coolant, then had it in the shop the next day. I've always made sure my vehicle was good to go ever since. **Tip:** Keep a receipt of everything you purchase for your vehicle: Gas, oil, brakes, tune ups, etc. All of these expenses are considered maintenance and can be written off as a business expense!

Make sure you have enough room in your vehicle to comfortably transport everything from home to gig to home. After packing your DJ equipment multiple times, you will have a usual routine, so packing your vehicle will become much easier to organize. When arriving at your event locations, always make sure you park close to doorways and entrances. If you are not parked close to the entrance and exit, you will have a harder time setting up and taking down, believe me. **Tip:** Kindly ask the event organizers to help you get premier parking. You will be surprised at how accommodating they will be!

The laptop. Most DJs I know use Apple products for their DJ businesses. Personally, I would prefer a PC-based laptop computer because I used to create my flyers and promotions on my Photoshop software on the same device. Today, (although I am retired from the business), I have an Android phone, so my computer and my DJ gear work together very well for me. If you are an "Apple person", you will love how everything integrates into DJ software quite easily. Also, having a good, fast, reliable laptop is great for processing software updates and quickly fixing compatibility issues with your controller. I once purchased a controller but had to return it because my laptop was too "advanced" for the technology. With due diligence, you will learn what works for you rather quickly. I also suggest having a good laptop bag/case. DJs usually work within large crowds and are surrounded by a lot of people drinking alcohol, so you want your DJ bag/case to be durable enough to handle the accidents you never saw coming. I would also suggest you tag your bag/case with a marker, sticker, logo, etc. to identify it in the dark or next to other DJ equipment. Those DJ booths can be pretty dark!

The DJ software is how your music files communicate with the controller (or mixer) so you'll want the best. For years, I was using a special video DJ software for my business. I liked it because I was mixing videos at a sports bar most weekends. So, the dance floor was able to see the videos on the TVs in the bar. It was pretty cool. But, since I stopped playing videos, I have switched over to the Serato software. Most DJs I know use it. At the time of publishing this book, Serato Lite (a shortened version) was free. This is great for beginners. Once you get the hang of it, I suggest you purchase the full subscription, and you will have a better time navigating. Either way, find the best software for yourself and your gear, and get familiar with it to help create smooth DJ sets. Use what you are most comfortable with.

Your controller is how you physically interact with your music. Your controller allows you do the mixing, scratching, and applying the effects onto the songs you play. There are plenty of options for you to choose from but stay mindful about what you want to spend on buying one. Do not spend money on the fancy features, or the controllers with the extra lights and buttons. You don't need it! Remember, your main objective is to learn how to master DJing parties before anything else. The fancy equipment happens later. Also remember that the DJs you see with the high-powered controllers have had years and years of experience and can afford to spend thousands to help them with their sets. You aren't there…yet.

The backup table. The locations and venues you get booked for may not have a table. It's important to prepare for this. Sometimes, the location may have a table, but it might be rusty, ripped up, broken, or wobbly. As a professionally prepared DJ, you will want to have a sturdy, foldable table in your car, ready to go at any time. **Tip:** Place a professional-looking table skirt on your table to impress your client!

The external drive is arguably the most important part of your DJ gear overall. It's the money maker that holds your music files! Not only that, having an external drive helps your computer perform better because it uses its own power to run. This means your computer doesn't have to use its own power to find your music. This can be critical if you own an older computer. Whether it is a solid-state external drive or a standard external drive, you want to carry and always keep this close to you. **Tip:** Remember that "Good things aren't cheap and cheap things aren't good." Spend the extra dollars to get the better external drives on the market. The very last thing any DJ wants to lose is access to their music. It happened to me. I accidentally dropped my external drive, and it stopped working. Because I didn't have a backup drive at the time, it took hundreds of dollars (and weeks of personal anguish and anxiety) to get it back. The company I hired to recover the drive only recovered about 80% of my 4TB drive. The awesome collection of music videos I had collected over the years were lost forever. Ugh!

Your powered speakers. Powered speakers are a mobile DJs best friend. They eliminate the need for a powered amplifier which means less equipment to carry around. Powered speakers allow you to be able to raise the music volume but still maintain great quality at all times. They are exactly what you will need to get your gigs done right. For years, I relied on 2 Mackie 15" powered speakers. They were able to handle a party for over 400 people! I strongly suggest you visit an actual DJ store and listen to the speakers before you buy. Make sure you can distinguish every instrument playing inside of every song! Make sure the store clerk pushes them babies to their limits to make sure they can handle the songs you want to play. No one, not even the party guests who have had a lot to drink, wants to hear bad quality music.

Disco light/laser lights. I would suggest you bring at least one disco light to your events. It adds another dimension to your DJ set. The light should be able to fill the venue, and it should be super easy to pack up. Your lights will add a dramatic flair to your gigs. Another alternative is to have a few lighted "towers". These are typically stand-alone lights that look great next to your DJ booth or table. It gives a great illumination to your DJ setup when the venue's lights are turned down. When a venue turns down the lights for people to dance, sometimes it becomes too dark to work. So, having your own lighting works well to help with the dance floor atmosphere and to help you light up your work area. too!

The Microphone. When DJing outdoor events and corporate functions, I liked to use wireless mics. For other events, I would rather use microphones with a long cord. In my experience, the person talking on the mic would get comfortable speaking and begin to walk freely through the venue. This situation can become very uncomfortable (and most times annoying) to everyone in the room, especially if the person speaking has a had a few beverages beforehand. I personally think having a mic with a long cord, reminds the person speaking (subconsciously) that they only have a few feet to work with as opposed to being able to walk freely. This also helps the speaker keep their speech short and keep them in everyone's view for pictures. Your client may expect you to have a wireless mic, so it's up to you to decide which option to offer as a service. Make sure you are clear about the microphone option when creating your contracts because really good wireless mics are expensive.

Your clothes. Your "uniform" or the clothes you wear affects your branding. Always bring 2 sets of clothes. The first set of clothes is how you arrive to the event. You need to look clean and comfortable, never forgetting about how people will perceive you. Do <u>not</u> wear items with holes, or items that may be perceived as "street wear". If you don't care about how you look, trust me, no one else will care, either. You will be meeting the venue staff and possibly the event organizers as soon as you arrive, so it is important to look great as you move your equipment. The weather can put a damper on loading and unloading, so you need to appear presentable regardless of the weather. After you finish setting up your DJ gear, use the restroom to clean yourself up and to change out of the 1st set of clothes and into the 2nd set of clothes. The 2nd set of clothing is for you to show up, show out, and showcase your business! You need to look your absolute best. Again, this is a part of branding you do not want to ignore. When you look great, the music sounds great, everything is going smoothly, and everyone is having a great time, your DJ brand elevates to new heights!

Backup equipment is critical to your reputation as a DJ. If your equipment breaks down and you do not have a backup, your DJ life is practically over. Always have a backup of everything. Speakers, cords, microphone, clothes, power strips, music, even your laptop. It's very likely you won't ever use your backup gear, but the one time you don't bring your backups, that is the time your equipment will have a problem.

I once DJ'd a Wedding for about 350 people in another state (California). The venue did not have a good space for me to work in. I was confined to a tiny space against a wall, near the entrance. I had just 2 feet of space to move around in. As the dance music was playing, I went to step over my mixer cord, and I accidentally pulled the cord out of the mixer. Oops! The music stopped and everyone in the place began staring at me. Embarrassing! I was able to reset with my backup mixer within a few minutes and the party continued. Can you image what would have happened if I didn't have backup equipment?

Chapter 5

Developing Your DJ Skills

Practice, Practice, Practice

Nothing will be more helpful to your DJ career than to practice. Learn to perfect your DJ skills as much as possible.

"Amateurs practice until they get it right, professionals practice until they can't get it wrong." - **Unknown**

There may be times when you'll be nervous or get a little anxious before your larger gigs, so you'll need to create the right environment that allows you to practice your DJ tricks and build your DJ style until you become flawless. Practicing your sets will help you get through these nerves with confidence. Keep in mind that being nervous is normal, no matter how experienced you are. Practicing also includes putting together a solid playlist for your next event. Thinking about your song choices before your gigs should be a part of your routine practice sessions. Another good way to practice for upcoming gigs is to invite a few buddies over to get on your equipment and play some music for each other. Use this time to take pics and video for awesome social media content. **Tip:** Join the various DJ social media groups to get more tips and techniques and add them into your practice sessions. Never stop developing your skills!

Reading The Crowds

The best DJs know how to read the room. One of my golden rules when DJing was to never play the same song twice. This helped me to expand my music libraries, it enabled me to carefully pick the songs I would play, and it allowed me to build up the party atmosphere. The crowd is expecting to hear dance music, so obviously you will want to play good dance music. Save the real "bangers" (favorites) for when you want to take the party to the higher levels. You can start reading any crowd by noticing the "toe-tappers", "head bobbers", or the people who like to dance in their chairs. These are your party starters! Once you get these people onto the dance floor, you are halfway there. Now, it's up to you to find the right songs to slowly add to the dance floor crowd. You must learn how to read the energy with every song you play. Once you pack the dance floor, it's time to launch the music they came to hear. Strategically mix in the bangers and watch the crowd get crazy!

Another great way to learn how to read crowds is to find a few good DJs on social media and send a direct message asking for some pointers. Ask how they do it. However, the very best way to learn how to read a room is to "shadow" a DJ and watch how they do it live. I suggest watching a good DJ work the crowd. If you witness a song that doesn't work with the crowd, figure out why. If you see a song that works, take note and learn how they transition into it and then out of it. Watch the crowd, feel the music, and feel the energy the DJ is creating. You may want to incorporate that style into your set, or you may think about doing it a completely different way. Either way, pay attention and always remember to feel the energy of the crowd because this is where the magic happens.

Handling Song Requests

In my experience, when the event is going great, this is typically when a person from the crowd will want to request a song. You will need to accept that some people will want to request songs when they are feeling good, so just take it as a compliment. The song they request may break the vibe you have going, or it may add to the fun, so play requests at your discretion! I once turned down a $100 tip to play a special song because I knew it would kill the party's vibe. A good way to handle someone coming to talk to you is to make eye contact, hold up your index finger, and signal "Hold On". Make your transition, make sure your next songs are ready to go, make sure you can give them a few seconds, then give that person your attention. **Tip:** Never allow anyone to ruin your rhythm and flow because they want to interrupt. I suggest making them wait to talk to you, and only when you are ready!

Your Playlists

I always knew my music and knew what worked and what didn't. I knew when it was time to "light it up" based on the crowd's behavior. So, be careful when you come to your sets with a playlist. Your pre-determined playlist tells me that you have already carved your roadmap for the event without knowing what the crowd wants. I'm not a fan of playlists because if you are in the middle of your playlist and the crowd isn't feeling it, why would you continue to go through the rest of your pre-determined song choices? My strategy was always about the crowd and the energy of the event. If the crowd wasn't feeling it, I would always switch it up or transition into a new direction. Your job is to build the energy and the vibe of the room at its highest levels, so change it up when you need to. **Tip:** If the crowd isn't feeling your playlist, change it up, then return to that playlist later, picking up where you left off. It may be a timing issue. It may be that you were coming in too hot, and the crowd just wasn't ready for it yet. Learn to read the crowd to know when they are ready for your skills!

When you're the "opening DJ", reading the crowd doesn't apply here because you don't have a crowd yet. People are still arriving to the venue. In that case, use this time as practice! Put together a few mashups you've been thinking about trying. Transition an old song with a newer one. Try new things while people are starting to get their drinks and working their way to the dance floor. No one is really paying attention, so this is always a good time to experiment with your music. Just don't get out of line with what you like to play because the people coming in will hear the craziness. Your job is to keep them engaged. You don't want them to walk out.

Chapter 6

Setting Up The DJ Business

Legalities

There is plenty of information via websites and online videos that can properly guide you to start a business. This Chapter is to help guide you lay the foundation for a DJ business, specifically. There are many risks involved when starting a business, so you must be absolutely sure of your intentions to run a legitimate business before you take on the risks.

Your first step in setting up a legal entity is to apply for your business license (online or in person). Each state is different, so visit your state's "business services department" and satisfy the requirements to obtain the proper license to operate. Get your State and Federal EIN numbers so your business can properly file its official records. If you acquire an accountant, hire one who has experience working with DJ companies or event companies. A good accountant can help you obtain your tax account numbers for you, if needed. Next, open a business bank account (so you can cash checks and have money sent to you in your legal business name). Having your tax account numbers will make opening a business bank account much easier.

Hire a lawyer. Hire one that understands the DJ business. There are so many variables when DJing various events, so having a good attorney on your side will protect you from any unexpected (or frivolous) lawsuits. Next, find a good insurance company that will insure you and your DJ equipment with at least $1 million in liability coverage... You will be glad you did (so will your attorney). It doesn't cost very much. Good coverage will cover you, your client, and in some cases, their guests. Also, you will be able to write off your insurance, gas, repairs, etc. as business expenses, so keep your receipts in a dedicated file folder to help stay organized. Lastly, be aware of any other special permits you may need within your state. Setting the right foundation is key to the success of your new business!

Your pricing. When it comes to offering pricing for your clients, most DJs typically offer 3 choices. They can charge a flat fee, they can offer packages, or they charge per service. My clients loved paying my flat fee because it eliminated the "nickel and dime" approach to charging clients for every single bit of activity. I always felt that if I am the DJ for the event, I should be responsible for everything within my control. So, I never charged extra for doing the basic tasks of my job. My clients also appreciated the simplicity of payment. The 2nd

option for charging your DJ services is offering a variety of packages. This gives the client options to book your services. This works well for Weddings because most Wedding budgets vary. Wedding couples are usually looking to get the most for their money, so they are usually very careful about what they are paying for. Helping the couple make wise decisions always works in your favor! The 3rd way DJs charge clients is to offer pricing per service. This works well when you have multiple services to offer like photo booth rentals, photography options, and Ministry services, for example. If you can offer additional services effectively, generate that additional income!

Creating Contracts

At the beginning of my DJ career, I was able to lock in gigs with a very simple approach. Whenever I spoke to the event organizers, I would explain to them that I would be most concerned with 4 basic things. I called them the "4 P's". It stands for:

- **People** (Guests) - I needed to know how many people were expected at each event so I can immediately know how much equipment I need to bring. If I needed to bring extra equipment or staff, I charged extra.
- **Power** - Where do I plug in? Is there an outside setup? Do I bring a generator? There were times when I would set up in a "rarely used" part of a venue/location that would force me to bring extra-long extension cords. Also, setups outdoors rarely have electrical power nearby, so I would need to bring a generator to power the gear. Remember, most people who plan

their events outdoors *never* think about how the power is being supplied!

- **Protection** - I always needed to know if my equipment will be protected. If it rains, I need my DJ gear to be 100% protected. I also need protection from the sun beating down onto my equipment. If there is a storm expected, I want to make sure I am not far away from my car to pack up quickly and safely. Make sure there is a tent (or enclosed booth of some kind) to protect your gear. When meeting with potential clients, if you feel that the protection for your DJ equipment is not being addressed appropriately and with respect, turn down the gig. Risking your equipment for any gig is not worth the trouble, no matter how much they are paying.

- **Price** – Find out what the client is willing to pay (or what their budget is) for your services. Most DJs undervalue their services. It took a long time for me to understand what my true value was. In the beginning of my DJ career, I would under-charge for my services just to secure the gig. DJs do this all the time. I would charge clients a low price to secure a Wedding and later see that the Dessert Table at the event was more expensive than my entire service! So, I learned to properly price myself at market value, nothing less. I learned if a client is only concerned with price, that person is not my client. Remember your worth! **Tip**: You may want to make a golden rule and stick to it. Say to yourself, "I will never accept a gig for less than $\_\_\_\_\_.$" Remember that there will always be cheaper DJs, and never forget that there are clients out there willing to pay for the value you can bring. Confidently stand tall on your pricing!

After you find out the 4P's, and agree to their requests, you can begin to write an official contract. The contract you create for your clients is a binding legal document. Create a contract that protects you and specifically outlines your services for each event. My biggest suggestion here is to make the contract simple and easy to understand. Longer contracts should be explained in detail before either party decides to sign. Also, from a marketing and branding standpoint, I would include items that your competition will not (or cannot) guarantee.

Here is a sample of things your competition may not be able to promise clients:

- Music for the event will be turned on at 6:00 p.m., guaranteed.
- The DJ we promised for your event will be the DJ for your event. (No switching last minute.)
- Lighting, wireless mic, and Master of Ceremony services are included in the final price.
- We will not charge extra for gas, mileage, and transporting equipment up and down flights of stairs.

Adding these items to your contract can be used as your branding strategy and will definitely help you stand out from your competition.

GOOD TIMES

AGREEMENT

Date: _____

Name: _____ Contact: _____

Address: _____

City: _____ State: _____ Zip Code: _____

Office Phone: _____

Other Phone: _____

E-mail address: _____

Event Date: _____ Hours of DJ Service (from/to): _____

Event Location: _____

Address: _____

City: _____ State: _____

Light Show?: _____

Wireless Microphone?: _____

Service Fee: $350.00

GOOD TIMES agrees to perform music entertainment at the above special event, during the hours shown above. Total service fee is $ 350 . (Please consider $100 per additional hour for overtime.) Receipt of the non-refundable deposit validates this contract and secures the reservation for the above date and hours. *Balance due is $_____ payable at event start.*

Please make all checks payable to: Rene' Velazquez

Good Times

Rene' Velazquez
_____   _____
Rene' Velazquez   Date

Chicago, IL 606

Director of Operations

(312)

_____   _____
Special Event Representative   Name Printed

The image above is one of my 1st DJ contracts. I created this when my DJ journey began. It's not pretty, but it worked. Whenever I met with clients (in person or on the phone), I would ask specific questions about each gig. I took that information and typed it into the fields later. My clients appreciated this simple document because it stood out from my local competition. My clients would sign a copy of the contract agreement and hand me the deposit. **Tip:** Securing a Deposit for your gigs is an absolute must! Many times, you can ask for 50% down, or you can ask for the full payment before the event date. If they cannot secure the Deposit, do not commit to the gig, period.

Start Your Part-Time Business

Many DJs that decide to create contracts for their services do well by contracting with schools, banquet halls, state fairs, festivals, coffee shops, etc.. So, creating a part time DJ business may work perfectly to supplement your income. Other DJs may feel they want the flexibility of having weekends and holidays set aside for family. In any case, you may feel comfortable working part time in your business and maintaining your freedom to do what you want. Speak to your accountant about the pros and cons regarding working your DJ business as a part-time entity because there may be added benefits to operating your DJ business part time! If you want to drive on into a full-time DJ career, I suggest you learn the art of DJing Weddings and Bar/Bat Mitzvahs. Weddings are the more complex than any other event but pay very well. (Bar Mitzvah and Bat Mitzvahs are a very close second.) My suggestion is to learn the ins and outs of Weddings so your DJ business can elevate to levels it is truly capable of.

NOTES

Chapter 7

Starting A Wedding DJ Business

Weddings Are Different

This Chapter is the largest because it is my favorite. I created a great living DJing Weddings for clients, so I'd like to give you as much information I can to help. Becoming a great Wedding DJ can be the most lucrative opportunity for you. Weddings are different from other events because there is so much more planning that happens for it to be successful. This is why most Weddings are usually planned months in advance. Many Wedding couples opt to hire a planner to help execute the event because the planning can be quite overwhelming. The most extravagant Weddings will likely cost tens of thousands of dollars and will likely be held at very prestigious locations. To have success DJing Weddings, you will need to be at the very top of your game. You must be great on the mic, you must be good at handling pressure, your DJ sets must be nearly flawless, and you must be able to create an event the Wedding couple will never forget. This Chapter will help you begin to construct your Wedding event services.

The Wedding DJ industry is very competitive. So, it is very important for you to separate your company from your competition. The biggest differentiator between my DJ company and my competitors was meeting each client, face-to-face. Word-of-mouth advertising about my business was excellent, so I would receive calls on a regular basis. I also had a good percentage of my business come from internet leads, so I would arrange an in-person meeting with every inquiry. Website visitors who chose not to meet with me, were never booked because I only wanted to work with couples who were willing to get to "know, love, and trust" me. I did not have an office, so I would meet my potential clients at a local restaurant or in my home. At the meeting, I learned the details of the event, but most importantly, I would ask more personal questions of the Wedding couple. I needed to know more information like how they met, where they grew up, their music preferences, and some of the ideas they had to make their event as special as they have always dreamed of. This information was key to constructing an amazing Wedding event tailored to them.

Construct The Perfect Wedding Gig

I've always felt the best way to honor the Bride and Groom was to give them a truly unique experience. An experience they will never forget. I used my father's method of planning each Wedding event from scratch and I want to share this with you.

I've always understood the careful planning and execution of each event was something to honor and cherish, just like the vows the Bride and Groom give to each other... unique and special. The technique I will share with you is how my father would help construct Wedding events with each Wedding couple. There are plenty of "DJ Wedding Templates" for creating a Wedding event, but the technique I will be sharing with you is one that has served me well and has created some of the best times of my life. Feel free to use this strategy or adapt it to something you would feel more comfortable doing. Either way, I hope it helps you plan Wedding events more carefully and helps you provide the very best service possible!

The Meeting

I started every Wedding event meeting (with the Wedding couple and/or Wedding Planners) with 2 blank sheets of paper. I would take one sheet of paper and start the meeting by writing the start time (near the top of the sheet) and the end time (near the bottom of the sheet). Then I would explain to the Wedding couple that my intention is to create a Wedding for them that is truly a one-of-a-kind event! I would start by asking basic questions like the Wedding Day, date, location, time start and finish, number of guests, etc. As the Wedding couple relays the information, I would write down the details. **Tip:** Never forget that this should be a conversation between yourself and the couple and not a "data capture". (You can do data captures with an email.) During your meeting, encourage the couple to talk as much as possible.

Learn to ask the couple questions that show you care. Ask how the couple met, where they grew up, why the couple picked that specific date, insert your experiences with the venue, ask about the (out of town) guests, etc. This is how you begin to bond with your client! **Tip**: This is also a great time to get the phone numbers you need: The Bride, Groom, Wedding planner or anyone else in charge of the event. In case an emergency arises, you will need more than 1 phone number to reach out. Keep these numbers in a safe place!

Using the left side of the 1st sheet, write down some of the items that occur during typical Weddings like this:

- Ceremony
- **Reception**
- Introductions
- 1st Dance
- The Toasts
- The Blessing
- **Dinner**
- Cake Cutting
- **Dessert**
- Mother/Son, Father/Daughter dances
- Bouquet/Garter Toss or Dollar Dance or Games
- **Dancing**

1st Blank Sheet of Paper

Ceremony? (yes or no)

Reception Start: 5:00pm

Day:_____
Date: _____
Time:_____

Introductions:

1st Dance:

Toasts:

The Blessing:

Dinner: 6:30pm

Cake Cutting:

Dessert: 7:15pm

Mother/Son
Father/Daughter Dances:
Bouquet/Garter Toss:
Dollar Dance:

Dancing: Games: (yes or no)

Wedding End:

The Wedding couple will begin to see your vision as you create their perfect night. This strategy works as a true collaboration for the event because you aren't just creating their special day for them, you're creating this special event <u>with</u> them!

Near the top of the paper, write the word "Ceremony". Ask the Wedding couple where they are exchanging vows. A majority of Wedding couples will have their ceremony at a church or a religious venue of some kind. However, if your couple is planning on having a ceremony near or inside the reception area, you may be required to provide 2 setups. The 1st setup may be nearby a pond or lake, it may be held in a private location, or it can be performed at the Bride's childhood home. In any case, you will need to get the specifics if they are requiring your equipment to help perform the matrimony service. This 1st setup will be much smaller and more intimate than the usual setup inside the reception location, but you need to charge for the service accordingly. Many times, the 1st setup will be for you to provide classical music (or something very light and classy) and provide the microphone for the person providing the ceremonial services. **Tip:** Make sure you know the timing of the Bridal Party walking the aisles and make double and triple sure that you play the right songs at the right times... especially for the Bride!

Other times, the ceremony will be held at the same location as the reception. This is not considered 2 setups. However, you will be starting a few hours earlier than normal to help with the ceremonial services. You should charge your clients that extra time on the clock. They will understand that you are working and will need to be paid for the added service.

The 4 Phases of Wedding Events

Before we really begin to dive into the heart of the meeting, I must first explain the 4 major parts of every Wedding event because there are 4 different "phases" of music you need to provide for the guests. Here's how I break down the 4 phases of every Wedding event:

1. **Reception.** This is when everyone arrives to the event, so your music must have a "love theme". Ensure the sound is clean and that the volume is at a respectable volume level. The music must be upbeat/welcoming. Do <u>not</u> play slow songs here.

2. **Dinner.** This is the time to lower the volume a bit and begin to play strictly "love songs". The key here is not to play songs that will put the guests to sleep! If you have an extensive music library, I suggest you flex your music archives during dinner and watch people light up when you play one of their favorites.

3. **Dessert.** At this time, you must raise the volume back up and begin to play crowd favorites. This is not the dance party music; this is popular music to get people moving again. It reminds everyone that the party is about to begin!

4. **Dance.** This is where you do your thing! Volume goes up a bit more, and you begin to work your lights. Switch up the music genres and music styles throughout the night to help keep everyone at the party entertained and having a great time until the event ends.

Reception. During your Wedding meeting, let the couple know that you will be leaving your home (or DJ equipment location) at least 2 hours before the start time. Depending on the location, you should account for about 30 minutes travel time, then give yourself at least 1 hour to set up. That would give you at least 30 minutes to test equipment, adjust dials and lighting, and ensure that you and your DJ gear are ready to go! **Tip**: Always use the same song to test your equipment. It will help you hear any "weird" issues and you'll be able to correct them with no problem. It is such a great feeling to be ready for the night and to see people start to walk into the event hearing your great music at pleasant music levels.

The reception is a critical time of the event because it sets the tone for the night. Guests are arriving, looking their best (all makeup and hairdos intact), hugging, and kissing close friends and relatives. Everyone is alert and ready to celebrate. **Tip:** Ensure the couple that the music will be turned on and ready to go at the designated start time! This relieves the couple of some of the stress about whether you will be arriving late. Your job during Reception is to get the event going by playing "upbeat" love songs as the guests arrive. Do not play anything other than love songs with a nice beat! While the couple is greeting everyone walking into the venue, let them know that everyone walking in will be greeted with love songs that make them want to tap their toes or bob their heads. This is one of the ways to test the crowd. Keep an eye on the guests that dance their way into the venue! Below is a tiny sample of a few classic song titles that I would play to set the vibe for the evening as guests were arriving (depending on the crowd, of course):

- "Isn't She Lovely" by Stevie Wonder
- "Teenage Dream" by Katy Perry
- "Rock With You" by Michael Jackson
- "Suga Suga" by Baby Bash
- "I Want To Hold Your Hand" by The Beatles
- "Crazy Little Thing Called Love" by Queen
- "I Love Your Smile" by Shanice
- "Build Me Up Buttercup" by The Foundations
- "Treasure" by Bruno Mars (clean version)
- "Some Kind of Wonderful" by Grand Funk Railroad
- "This Kiss" by Faith Hill
- "Fantasy" by Mariah Carey
- "This Will Be (An Everlasting Love)" by Natalie Cole
- "More Today Than Yesterday" by Spiral Staircase
- "Fallen" by Mya (this is the song I would use to do my sound checks)
- "Roses Are Red" by Mac Band
- "Love Come Down" by Evelyn "Champagne" King

Introductions. Next, ask the couple to give you the names of all members of the Bridal Party. Do your best to get everyone's name and in the right order they will be announced. The Bride may not have her complete list ready at the time of the meeting, so just leave a space for a name when she confirms her list at a later date. Include the Flower Girl, the Ring Bearer, the entire Bridal Party, any parents, and ask the couple if they would like you to announce any out-of-town guests or any special family members during the introductions. Let the couple know that you will announce the bridal pairings with the words "escorted by" between the names. **Tip:** When writing the names down, the spelling does not matter but make absolutely sure you pronounce the names perfectly! Also, ask the couple which song the Bridal Party would like to come out to. It's one of the most exciting parts of the evening, so announcing the Bridal Party will need to be full of energy and excitement! I suggest you practice the introductions before the Wedding date because announcing the Bridal Party will need to be flawless.

Immediately after the Bridal Party, you will be introducing the Wedding couple. Ask the couple how they would like to be introduced. It could be "Mr. and Mrs. Smith". It could be "Mr. John and Mrs. Mary Smith". It could also be "Mr. and Mrs. John Smith". Make sure the future Bride and Groom agree on the way they'd like to hear their names. Also ask the couple what song they would like to enter the room with, keeping in mind that they will probably only hear about 20 seconds of the song before the crowd goes crazy! How I used to do it: I would make sure the Bridal Party introductions are complete. I would turn off the music, I'd politely ask the guests to stand and prepare to welcome the Bride and the Groom. (This allows time for everyone to get their phones out to record.) I hit the entrance music, I get the crowd fired up, and the Wedding couple enters the room! It's so much fun!

The 1st Dance. One way to ensure a very special first dance is to suggest that you would like the couple's 1st dance to happen immediately after introducing them to the guests. Tell the couple that after you announce them and after they enter the room, you will need them to stay in the middle of the dance floor. The reason you want to do this is because this the best opportunity to have the audience's full attention. The guests will have their cameras out, everyone will be applauding and cheering, and all of the guests will have their full attention on the Wedding couple. So, it's the perfect time to do the 1st dance and get it out of the way early. The photographers and the videographers will love you for this. This also gives the audience their best opportunity to take amazing pictures of the Wedding couple to share. Once the 1st dance ends, have the Wedding couple walk to their seats (to the head table) so the event can continue.

The Toasts. Next, ask the couple if the Maid of Honor and the Best Man will be giving toasts. Will they be making speeches? Who else would like to give a toast? These speeches are usually fun and unpredictable moments because 90% of the time the speakers aren't familiar with speaking in public. It can lead to some very memorable moments! The speeches can be done at the head table, or you can have them stand and deliver in front of your DJ booth/table. As they give their speeches, the kitchen should be ready to deliver the 1st course, usually starting with the salad. Try to get a signal from one of the servers to make sure the kitchen is ready. The Wedding couple already has a time they scheduled dinner to be served. Write it down. This is merely a "suggestion" because in my years of DJing Wedding events, dinner was served on time… once! This is normal. **Tip**: Do not worry so much about the timing of dinner. As long as the dinner is running relatively close to schedule, everything is ok. Wedding events rarely happen on schedule, so there is no need to stress. If the Wedding couple is happy and the guests are doing great, you're doing fine.

The Blessing of the food usually happens immediately after the toasts, so make double sure the kitchen is ready to serve before someone blesses the food. If there is a Pastor, Preacher, Minister, Priest, Officiant, etc. hired (or asked) to bless the food, have that person approach the DJ booth. Ask the couple to give you the name of the person blessing the food. (Most times, it's the person who directed the Ceremony.) Be sure to announce this person then let them proceed. The actual blessing should only take a minute or 2. When the blessing finishes, signal to the kitchen for the dinner service to begin. If everything is going well, the kitchen will bring out the 1st course right on time. As soon as the servers drop that 1st plate of food, dinner service begins.

Dinner. Many DJs don't pay much attention to this part of the Wedding event. Instead, most DJs like to play their same old "dinner music" playlist then disappear for a while. This is a huge mistake on their part! They are missing a golden opportunity to connect to the crowd. This is where I separated my DJ business from the rest! Firstly, as soon as the 1st dish is being served, the music must be toned down. Slightly turn down the volume (so the guests can communicate with each other) then begin to play softer love songs. There are millions of love songs that the Wedding couple and their guests would love to hear on their special day, so try to give them a mix of nice calming dinner music. "Wow" the guests by playing great music that adds a nice touch to the event. I always loved watching some of the guests sing along to the music during dinner because it meant that I "touched" their soul without ever meeting them… it's magical. Try to "surprise" the Bride by playing a few love songs that reminds her of the time they first met each other, and you will see the Bride light up with joy. **Tip:** Try not to play the super slow songs like "Unchained Melody" by the Righteous Brothers or "I Will Always Love You" by Whitney Houston because you will run the risk of putting the guests to sleep! Ensure the Wedding couple that you are committed to playing only great love songs. Depending on the crowd, here are a few of my favorite "must play classics" for dinner:

- "Chapel of Love" by The Dixie Cups
- "Que Sera Sera" by Doris Day
- "Sabor a Mi" by Eydie Gorme' y Los Panchos
- "Cruisin'" by Smokey Robinson
- "Leather and Lace" by Stevie Nicks and Don Henley
- "Forever and For Always" by Shania Twain
- "You Are" by Charlie Wilson
- "Show You The Way To Go" by The Jacksons
- "Love and Marriage" by Frank Sinatra
- "Amazed" by Lonestar
- "Gema" by Los Dandys
- "That's Amore'" by Dean Martin
- "Waiting For A Girl Like You" by Foreigner
- "L-O-V-E" by Nat King Cole

As you play during dinner, try your best not to sit and eat with the guests. The Wedding couple may have a dinner seat planned for you but explain to them that you need to work. **Tip:** Your job here is to look for the dancers in the group! In my experience, I would explain to the Wedding couple that I never eat dinner at receptions. This was intentional because one time I had gotten a little sick from a Wedding dinner. After I ate dinner with the guests, I was in and out of the bathroom all night! I never did it again. If I did have a seat for dinner, I only ate the bread and spread a little butter on it. So, if the Wedding couple insists that you sit with the guests, specifically request to sit with the photographer and videographer. Here is where you can "win friends and influence people". Quickly introduce yourself and your DJ business to the photo/video people, quickly go over the agenda for the evening, then tell them where to position themselves to get their "money shots" through the night. Not only will they appreciate your help, but the Wedding couple will also appreciate the amazing shots they'll have of their night as well. This is a great way to plant your business into their minds because there is a good chance you'll work with them again in the future. Trust me, the photographers and videographers have seen their fair share of bad DJs, so do your best to be the professional they want to work with! You will be amazed at the number of leads a good photographer can give you.

The Cutting of the Wedding Cake. The Wedding couple will need to eat dinner, of course, but suggest to the couple that they cut their Wedding cake during dinner while guests are still dining. Most times, the couple would rather do it without bringing much attention to themselves. They may opt to cut the cake off to the side with just a few guests and the photo/video person present. Other times, they may request that you announce it for everyone to see. If so, play a fun song, and cut the cake in the middle of the dance floor. Having the cake cut early is a good thing because the kitchen likes to have it ready for the guests who may choose to leave early. It also helps the kitchen eliminate another task on their long list of duties. Again, your photographer and videographer will appreciate you moving the event along. **Tip:** No one ever notices how well you're managing the schedule, so move the event according to your direction!

Dessert. Have the Wedding couple imagine that dinner is finishing, and dessert is now being served. Let the couple know that it's time to switch things up. You will be changing the music out of the "love song" theme and move into songs that the crowd will want to move to. To this point, everyone has been eating good food, having great conversations, drinking wine, etc., and they are getting more comfortable in their seats. Your job is to get them out of their comfort zones and get them ready to dance and celebrate. This is a huge challenge for any DJ! Turn the volume up a little bit and start to play something to shake them out of their chairs. Look for the "chair dancers" and the "toe tappers" in the crowd. These are your targets because these guests are usually the influencers of the audience. It's ok to turn the volume up a bit, so make sure the guests are finished with dinner before you move them into the next phase of the event. Depending on the crowd, I would shake up the crowd with a classic song like:

- "Pride And Joy" by Stevie Ray Vaughn
- "Here For The Party" by Gretchen Wilson
- "Life Of The Party" by Charlie Wilson
- "El Amor" by Tito El Bambino
- "Can't Stop The Feeling" by Justin Timberlake
- "Firecracker" by Josh Turner
- "A Night To Remember" by Shalamar
- "Dance With Me" by Michael Jackson
- "Bidi Bidi Bom Bom" by Selena
- "Suds In The Bucket" by Sara Evans
- "Call Me Maybe" by Carly Rae Jepsen
- "What a Fool Believes" by The Doobie Brothers
- "American Boy" by Estelle featuring Kanye West
- "Shake Your Body Down" by The Jacksons
- "Stomp!" by Brothers Johnson

Your goal is to get them dancing in their seats, bouncing on their way to the bar, singing along to the music, etc. **Tip:** Keep the vibe at this level because the dancing will officially be starting a few minutes after dessert is finished!

Mother/Son and Father/Daughter Dances. Next, ask the Wedding couple if they plan on executing these traditional dances. If so, make sure you note the names and the partner titles (mother, father, uncle, etc.). In my experience, the mothers and fathers don't like to dance the whole song, so this may be over with shortly. What you can suggest is to have them dance until after the chorus of the song, then softly end the song there. This strategy works because it gives the crowd a chance to take pictures, the meaning and symbolism stay intact, and it saves a bit of time. Again, the photographer, videographer, and the guests will thank you for moving things along.

Bouquet/Garter Toss or Dollar Dance. Ask the Wedding couple if they would like to do the traditional Garter removal and Bouquet Toss after the special dances. If so, this could be a good time to do it. However, I've had many couples choose to do it later in the evening. Remind the couple that you will instruct the photographer to take pictures of the person who caught the bouquet and the person who caught the garter. (Read how I conducted Bouquet and Garter Tosses, in detail, in the Bonus Chapter.) The Dollar Dance is very popular. It's where the Bride and Groom stand in the middle of the dance floor, separate from each other. The guests form 2 lines (one for the Bride, one for the Groom) and they wait in line to slow dance for a few seconds each. However, before they begin to dance, the guests will pin a dollar or more to the Bride's dress. The other line will pin a dollar or more to the Groom's suit. Depending on the amount of people waiting in line to dance, this can go on for a few songs.

Games. If there is a special performance or a game of some kind, it usually happens in this time slot. The "shoe game" is a good one. There is another game where the Wedding couple takes a photo at every table before a "fun" song runs out. There are many other popular games and family traditions to work with. If you have a game scheduled, or if there is a special performance scheduled, build it up the best you can to keep the momentum high. **Tip:** During the games or special performances is when you will need to have strong emcee skills. A good emcee can keep the energy high and keep the crowd happy and motivated.

Next, go over the dancing section of the event. Make sure you know when the dancing should start and what time you need to close out the evening. When it's time to start the dancing, most Wedding DJs reach into their bag of tricks to get the crowd up from their seats to dance. My suggestion for you is to try to stay "neutral" as long as possible! What I mean by staying neutral is to play for everyone at the event, not just for the younger dancers. It's expected that most of the older guests will want to leave early, but you don't want to "force" them out of the party. Most newer DJs tend to do this thinking that it's the best way to selfishly get to their dance music library. Wrong. The older guests want to have a good time, too! These guests were invited for special reasons, so honor them by playing a few songs they might enjoy hearing. Don't forget… the Wedding couple would love to see them on the dance floor! It can be a challenging task, but if you know music well, you should be able to maintain a healthy mix of music for everyone to enjoy throughout the night. If you learn to master this skill, you will never run out of work!

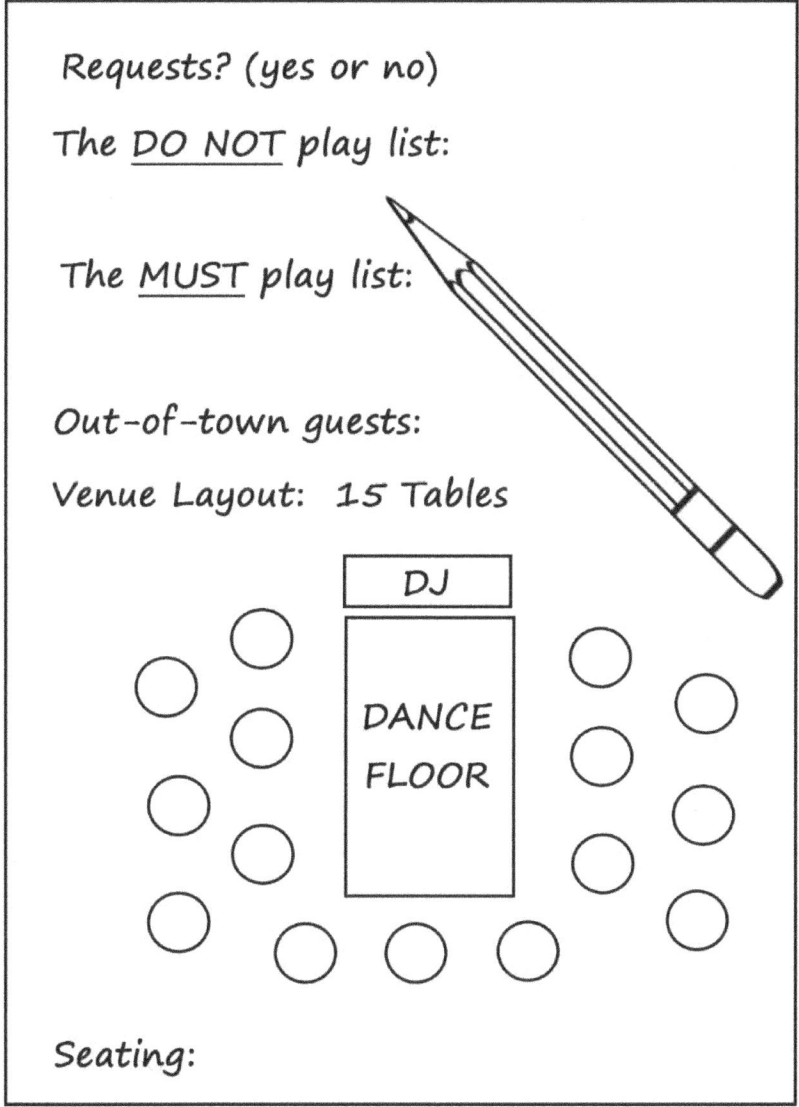

2nd Blank Sheet of Paper

Requests? (yes or no)

The <u>DO NOT</u> play list:

The <u>MUST</u> play list:

Out-of-town guests:

Venue Layout: 15 Tables

DJ

DANCE FLOOR

Seating:

The end of the Wedding meeting is near. Take out your 2nd sheet of paper. This sheet is needed to list a few more things before you can end the meeting. It's your job to make the couple feel assured that you've covered everything, so ask a few more questions like:

- Playing requests (Is this allowed? Is there someone specifically forbidden to request songs?)
- The DO NOT play list (There will be songs that the Bride and/or Groom will <u>not</u> want to hear on their Wedding Day. Do your best to keep this list short.)
- The MUST play list (Limit this list to about 5 or 10 songs! Remind the Wedding couple that you are not their personal streaming service, you are a professional DJ hired to create their wonderfully memorable event.)
- The out-of-town people (Would they like them to be acknowledged?)
- Venue Layout (Sketch the venue's floor plan then strategize your speaker placement)
- Seating charts (Let the Wedding couple know not to sit the elders near the speakers)

The information here will also act as part of your "cheat sheet" for the evening. You will definitely need a cheat sheet to keep the event on schedule and to make sure you are providing the service you had promised. Once you've completed this 2nd sheet, you should have the information (and confidence) needed to end the meeting.

End the meeting. Do this by going over the agenda, from start to finish. Ensure that their special night will go smoothly without any major issues. Have the new couple take a photo of your notes or let them know that you'll re-type them and send them later. You will be using these notes to draw up an official contract to sign. The Wedding couple will become terribly busy with other event planning, so get a date in their schedule to meet at least once more. The next meeting is when they will sign the contract and submit their Deposit (unless you have already done so). The Deposit is usually 50% of the total amount of your service. If they have already submitted their Deposit, explain that the 2nd meeting will be to pay the remaining balance before the event. Thank the Wedding couple for their time and escort them to their vehicle.

The 2nd meeting. Now that you have the basic outline of the event, it's time to put the agenda together. Take all the information you gathered at the meeting and type it up into your contract. **Tip:** Be very specific as to what your clients will expect for the entire event because this contract will also outline the exact services you will provide. Your contract should be written to protect both parties. You're now ready to present the contract at the 2nd meeting. This meeting will be short and sweet. Go over the details of the contract, ask the couple to sign the contract, and have them submit the deposit (if they haven't already). If there is a remaining balance, it is usually paid about a week before the event. **Tip:** Do your best to avoid having the balance paid on the day of the event. You don't want the Bride or the Groom to forget to pay you. They have enough to worry about! No matter how it's taken care of, make sure the balance is paid in full before you start playing any music!

The Cheat Sheet

Your cheat sheet is your complete game plan for the evening. It helps ensure everything goes smoothly throughout the night. Make sure you always keep the cheat sheet nearby and refer to it often. As things happen, check them off from the list. It's very important that you keep your eyes on the clock to ensure that the evening is moving along as you have planned it.

<u>NOTES</u>

Sample Cheat Sheet

4:00 – Reception/Cocktail Hour Begins

4:45 - INTRODUCTIONS
DJ plays "How Beautiful" – Twila Paris
DJ Announces:
Flower Girl – Mully Jimenez escorted by Samuel Ochoa
Ring Bearer - Blake
Bride's Parents – Benjamin & Amalia Negrete
Groom's Parents – Alan & Angie Stepper
DJ announces:

"Mr. & Mrs. Tracy & Ryan Stepper"!!
DJ Announces:
Cutting of Cake – Photo Op
DJ Plays Richard Elliott
Toast – Tony Flores
Prayer – Uncle Chris

5:00 – Dinner

6:00 - 1st Dance
DJ Plays "Then" – Brad Paisley

6:03 – Father/Daughter Dance
DJ plays "Walk With You " – Edwin McCain

6:10 – Dancing

8:00 – Dollar Dance
DJ plays "Journey/Billie Jean Mix"

9:00ish - Bouquet Toss/Garter Throw
DJ Plays "fun" music for happenings

Special Songs:
"Crazy Girl" – Eli Young Band
"Making Memories Of Us" – Keith Urban

YES!!

Reggaeton	1950's	Cha Cha Slide
Motown	Old School	Freestyle
"Fantasy Girl"	Katy Perry	Disco

NO!!
CURSING

Justin Bieber	**"Macarena"**	**Michael Bolton**
"Y.M.C.A."	**Rap**	**"Chicken Dance"**

Chapter 8

Managing And Growing Your Business

Enjoy The Journey

At this point in your DJ career, you should be doing well. You are booking gigs regularly and you are mastering your techniques. You are reading crowds, you are in complete command or your dance floors, and you know what to play 3, 4, or 5 songs ahead of time. On social media, people are watching you, they are enjoying your content, and they are commenting and sharing your posts. Also at this point, you are packing and unpacking your equipment so well that you can do complete setups and takedowns in less than 30 minutes! Family and friends are always asking for you to DJ their events, but you are just too busy (honestly!). This is such a great time in your DJ career. You can cruise through your gigs with supreme confidence. Enjoy it. Embrace it. It took a lot of time, energy, mistakes, and effort to get to this point, so pat yourself on the back for getting this far. Now is the time to think about expanding your business to higher levels. To do that, we will need to have some sort of system in place.

Building Your Marketing Campaigns

The #1 tried and true way for any business (in any industry) to increase business is by word-of-mouth. What people are saying and thinking about your company and your brand is critical to your success. It is very important that you set a marketing system in place to consistently gain new business contacts. What I would do in the past was send a self-addressed stamped envelope to my client after every gig or event. Inside was a basic form asking to rate the different aspects of the event. From music selection, to lighting, to emceeing, etc., I was interested in knowing what my clients thought about the service I provided. At the bottom of the form, I asked to list 2 or 3 people who would benefit from services. I was always surprised by the number of people who responded and gave me names of new leads. Unfortunately, the self-addressed stamped envelope is a thing of the past. Today, I would suggest you create your own QR Code and have it posted on your DJ table at each event. When people click on it, they are taken to a contact form to add their name, phone number, etc. To make it more interesting, offer a chance to win a Free Party if they enter their information. Experiment with different strategies (a discount, a free service, etc.) to gain more business.

Another idea would be, after each event, send an email to your client with a survey asking to rate the services you had provided. The key here is to be specific. Ask about your arrival time, your professionalism, the guest feedback, the flow of the event, etc. At the end of the email, ask for any referrals they may have. There is no better time to ask for a referral!

Corporate marketing. Any business in any industry has "peaks and valleys", highs and lows. If your DJ business hits a low cycle and you want to ensure a steadier flow of business, you may want to reach out to the corporate world. Target the people who would be more apt to hire you… the event organizers. Seriously consider attending free business networking events so you can engage with C-level executives face-to-face. Whether it be an annual celebration, a Holiday tradition, or a new product launch, every company has an event coming soon. If there is a fee to join these networking groups or events, you may want to consider paying the fee, if your budget allows. Local Chambers of Commerce and other networking groups tend to meet regularly. This is such a great way to network with community leaders. Have your awesome business cards ready! If all goes well, you will open doors and book more high-paying gigs!

Email marketing. To make my point regarding email marketing I will need to take a sidestep into the business world. Let's look at the devastation of small businesses during the Covid-19 pandemic from 2020 to 2023. The United States government mandated that all small businesses temporarily shut down. This resulted in millions of small businesses being forced to close permanently. If the owners of the businesses didn't contract Covid, nor did the employees, why did these companies go out of business? Here's why: These businesses were used to regular customer traffic, but the business never captured their customer's personal information! They never knew their customer's name, email, phone, address, etc. so they weren't able to communicate or promote the business effectively. You, however, have the opportunity to communicate with your clients because you have this information. My suggestion is to keep open communication with your clients. Send them a newsletter. Send them a link to your website. Let them know what's happening with your business by keeping them engaged. **Tip:** Never stop building your customer list! There are quite a few email marketing companies that can help you and your business maintain communication with your customers. Many times, the service charge is just a few dollars per month. If you're able to generate one extra gig with email marketing, you may be able to pay the cost for the entire year!

Chapter 9

Long-Term Success In The DJ Industry

Never Stop Learning

There is a very small percentage of DJs that take their love of the DJ business to the highest level of the industry. These are the DJs that have a thriving DJ company and have multiple DJs working for them. They may have at least 3 events going at the same time and have more than 4 DJs (and helpers) working on the same night. If you are aspiring to get to this point, know that DJs with large companies all have 1 thing in common: A smart Customer Relationship Management (CRM) software program. This program will help in planning events, capturing data, sending Invoices, scheduling, and helping with the day-to-day operations of the business. With technology moving at a lightning pace, CRM systems are becoming easier to operate and more inexpensive in the market. Look carefully into purchasing a robust CRM system (for DJs) that works well with your business goals and objectives.

As a full-time DJ business owner, never forget that you must stay committed to creating great memories for each event. Your clients will always be the focal point of your business and making them your priority is the key to staying in business. Learn what your clients want by managing their requests, listening to their concerns, and adapting to their last minute changes.

Also keep in mind that the DJs working for you may have concerns and issues like flat tires, equipment failure, money disputes, conflicts with clients, and so much more. My suggestion is to grow your business slowly so you can learn to handle these types of problems. Growing too big, too fast has been the downfall of many great DJ companies! When you put a good system in place and have great DJs working for you, there is nothing that can stop your success!

Advanced Systems

I once met a billionaire and asked, "What is the key to making millions of dollars?" He explained that all you need to do is create a system. It does not matter what you sell, just make sure you have a system in place to sell it. Once you have a good system in place (one that is very efficient and has very few problems or issues), you duplicate it. Duplicating that business creates a new set of issues. The next step would be is to eliminate the "bugs" from this new system. Once you've done that, duplicate your system again. Continue to duplicate your systems until you have reached your goal. That's it! It seems easy to do, but there is an incredible amount of work that goes into building a successful business. You will need to create a few new systems to build a successful DJ business. Namely, you will need a marketing system and a customer relationship system.

Marketing Systems

Your marketing system for your DJ business is a main component to your overall DJ business. When a potential client calls, texts, or contacts your business, you must have a plan to convert the contact into a sale or a contract for a new gig. Most people expect a business to respond to their inquiries within 24 hours, so it is critical to build a system to respond to client inquiries and customer requests immediately. If you don't, your competitor will. Consider paying for a type of answering service to ensure you do not miss calls. When a customer emails or fills out a Contact Form from your website or landing page, you should have an automatic response going directly back to the person who made the contact. Make sure you monitor these costs very carefully. You do not want to put unnecessary dollars into campaigns that don't work.

Another tip to winning new clients is to purchase a booth at Bridal Shows. At Bridal Shows, Brides-to-be are shopping for Wedding services, so there are usually plenty of DJ companies that exhibit their DJ services at these shows. The competition is fierce! I suggest attending these bridal shows *before* you decide to purchase a booth because you will need to see how other DJ companies are winning new clients. Maintaining professionalism is the key to winning new clients, especially at these shows.

Another way to market your business and to generate leads is to have your business listed on websites dedicated specifically to Wedding vendors and services. These websites give you the opportunity to post your logo, your contact information, and post a good description of your business. A good profile here can really increase your customer base, but again, monitor your expenses to ensure the price is worth the effort. It may cost a few dollars per month to display your information, but this is what the more established DJ companies are doing. It's how they stay at the top of the industry. It's where you want to be.

Also consider joining an industry-wide association strictly for DJs. There are many of them available, so make sure you are joining the associations that are highly accredited and have reputable DJ companies as members. Joining these types of groups is always good to help take your DJ business to higher levels. They put on DJ-only events and conferences throughout the country. They also have world-renowned DJs speak at many of their conferences, giving tips and sharing their experiences in the DJ world. Networking with the other top-caliber DJ companies from other parts of the country may have advice to help you land top gigs in your area!

Customer Relations

The other leg of your overall system is the customer relationship system. This is how you should expect to nurture and appreciate your clients because it helps separate your company from your competition. In my experience, most people who hire DJs don't have much expectation of the DJ company they choose. This can become a great opportunity to dazzle them! Take your business to higher levels by communicating with your clients effectively and giving them stellar communication. Always be clear about details so that your client never has to ask you basic questions. After each conversation with your client, be clear about the next steps toward creating an amazing event.

Another way to stay in the minds of your clients is to send an unexpected treat. Send a personalized birthday card, give out refrigerator magnets, giveaway calendars every year, send flowers on Wedding anniversaries, or invite your clients to an exclusive invite-only Holiday party! Stay in their minds and they will "reward" your efforts with new business!

Get reviews! When you're comfortably connected to your customer base, you can ask for reviews with little effort. Your clients will be glad to help. It's hard to get reviews, so when you have the opportunity, get them! Make sure you direct your clients to websites and online review portals where people are likely to see the great reviews of your DJ business. Also, if you are able to ask your clients for testimonials... Fantastic! The best testimonials you can have are the ones captured on video. You can use these to post onto your social media channels, your website, and your landing pages. Another way to get the most value out of a video testimonial is to create your company presentations using the video clips. These video testimonies help your business' brand and credibility.

Bonus Chapter

Bonus Material

Prepare For Success

Operations of your DJ business is how you execute your service. When you are preparing for a gig, take some extra time to get your music together. Make sure the playlist is amazing. As the date gets closer, ensure your equipment is 100% functional and ready to go. The day before the gig, make sure you are filled up on gas, the tires have the right pressure, and your vehicle is running in top shape. On the day of the gig, try to have a specific plan to load up your DJ gear into the vehicle because it helps save time. After packing the vehicle, leave to the location at least 2 hours before your start time. When you arrive, find the best place to park. This is key because you will want to be as close to the venue as possible after your set. Your gigs can be exhausting!

The Wedding Rehearsal Dinner

Ask the Wedding couple if they intend on having a rehearsal dinner before the Wedding. Typically, a rehearsal dinner is strictly for close family members and the Bridal Party. As the DJ, you don't want to impose on the family's personal space, so ask the couple if it is possible to meet them toward the end of the dinner. Your objective here is to get a good idea of the venue. Note where you will park your car. Ask the staff where you will be loading and unloading your gear. Inside the venue, envision where you will set up and where you will set your speakers and lights. **Tip**: Ask the couple where they intend to sit their older guests. If their older guests are being seated near your speakers, do your best to get that arrangement changed! Warn them that you might get complaints through the night that your speakers are too loud, and you will be forced to play music at a volume lower than usual. Also, the guests who are sitting farthest from you will complain that they aren't able to hear the music. It can be a disaster! Another positive about attending the rehearsal dinner is that you may meet the Bridal Party. They will have so many ideas of song choices for you! The Bridal Party is usually a lot of fun. They will have you pumped up for the event!

Setting Up Your Sets

After you arrive to the venue and unload your vehicle, begin your set up inside. This should not take more than an hour. As you load your equipment, unpack your gear, set up your lights, etc. everyone working there is watching you. You will need to forget all about the bad weather, awful traffic, and leave your personal issues behind. Transform into your DJ persona and shine like a rock star! Have a consistent routine of doing your "sound checks" and "light checks" before you start to play. This includes powering up your laptop. Have your software updates installed to ensure the software is 100% ready to go. After the event, pack your vehicle and carefully drive back to the home base. If you can master these basic steps, you will learn to save time, energy, and a world of stress in your life.

Black Masking Tape

Always make sure you tape your cords to the floor, so people won't trip over them. My suggestion is to tape your cords from your gear, along the bottom of a wall, directly to your speakers and lights. Even if your speaker or lights are over 30 feet away from your gear, tape your cords so no one can see them! I always taped my cords to the floor in a way that they had minimal exposure to the general walking or dancing areas. The last thing you want to happen is a guest or a V.I.P. walking near your set and fall because you didn't secure your cords. Your DJ career can be ruined! Many DJs avoid this by using wireless or Bluetooth speakers. So, choose speakers you feel would be best for you and your situations.

Wedding Event "Headquarters"

Along with orchestrating the perfect Wedding event, please remember that you will also need to handle the tiny, unexpected emergencies that arise throughout the evening.

Never forget that the DJ is in charge of the event "headquarters" for the evening. Make sure you know the name of the venue's Manager, or at the very least, know the names of a few of the servers. The DJ table will be the unofficial "Lost and Found" area. If a car needs to be moved, the DJ will make the announcement. The DJ will need to know where the coat check is and other things like where the bathrooms are. Should any problems arise, the DJ will need to know how to resolve them quickly. It will be important that you also note these "miscellaneous" items onto your cheat sheet. It will help keep you grounded and on schedule.

Introducing The Bridal Party

When it is nearly time to introduce the Bridal party, I would gather the Bridal party and have them meet me in the staging area (usually the entrance hallway). I would line them up in the proper order and I'd make sure to pronounce every single person's name correctly! It is very important that each person's name is pronounced correctly because there is a good chance the whole family is there expecting you to say it right! Try to learn the nicknames (if any). When you get on the mic, make sure your voice is firm and clear as you ask everyone to their seats. Remember, your job is to guide this event so that everything run smoothly. Take charge.

Everyone's ready and in their places. Cue the Bridal Party music, hit play, then you should be able to introduce the Bridal Party with no problem. Make sure you bring the energy of the room to optimum levels. My suggestion is to call out the 1st name of the couple, say "escorted by", then say the other person's name. It sounds very classy this way. When you say the nicknames in the Bridal Party, the crowd loves it! **Tip**: If you don't want to play the same old classical music to introduce the Bridal Party, use one that is classy and has a little more "flair" to it. Here is a song that has never failed me:

- "Just You And Me" by Richard Elliott

Next, cue the entrance song for the Wedding couple. Ask everyone to stand. Hit play, then introduce the Wedding couple with excitement...The crowd goes wild!

The Bouquet/Garter Toss

Clear the dance floor. Have the Bride come to one end of the floor and ask the guests to bring all of the "single ladies" to the other end of the dance floor. Here are a few songs that would work well to get the single ladies to participate:

- "Man! I Feel Like A Woman" by Shania Twain
- "Single Ladies" by Beyonce'
- "Pretty Girls Walk" by Big Boss Vette

Have the single ladies congregate on the opposite side of the dance floor. Tell the Bride to turn her back to the ladies. On the count of 3 have the Bride throw the bouquet over her shoulder to the group of ladies. Have the photographer take the picture of the person who caught the Bouquet.

After the Bride throws her bouquet, it's the Groom's turn to throw the garter. But first, the Groom has to actually retrieve the garter. So, get a chair to the dance floor and place it on one side of the dance floor, typically the side to get the best picture. Have the Bride sit in the chair. Instruct the Groom to stand on the opposite side of the dance floor, facing his new Bride. Get everyone charged up to witness the event! Explain to the Groom that his job is to retrieve the garter from his beautiful Bride. Tell him he must start walking to the Bride when the music starts. But it can't be just any walk. It must be a sexy walk to the Bride. It must be <u>thee</u> walk that made her fall in love! Get back to the decks and hit play. The song you play should be:

"Let's Get It On" – Marvin Gaye

The men go crazy, and the Groom usually has a fun time with it. Once he retrieves the garter, it's the men's turn to catch the garter the same way the ladies caught the bouquet. Ask the guests to bring the "single men" to the dance floor. Here is the song I would play to get the guys fired up to participate:

"Who Let The Dogs Out?" - The Baha Men

Have the Groom facing with his back to the single guys. On the count of three, have the Groom throw the garter. Once the garter has been secured, get the "garter catcher" and the "bouquet catcher" together. Have the photographer get a picture of the 2 "winners".

Party Starter

Start the party! I had an amazing Wedding technique to get the party going and I want to share it with you. I have used this technique for so many couples and their families for so many years. When I needed it, it worked every... single... time. I think part of the success of this trick is the fact that the Bride and the Groom never knew it was coming. To start, I would either stand on a chair or move to the center of the dance floor and ask for everyone's attention. I would then ask the Bride and the Groom to come to the middle of the dancefloor. They never knew what was happening! The photographer and videographers are there, capturing the moments. Next, I would ask everyone to join them by creating a giant circle around them. This would take a few minutes because not everyone had plans on ever touching the dance floor. So, I would ask the Bride and the Groom to help me by calling out some names of the people who were still sitting in their seats. If you are good on the mic, you can throw in a joke or 2 to keep everyone laughing and in a great mood.

Everyone is now in a circle and the Bride and Groom are in the center. I get back on the mic and say, "Ladies and Gentlemen, I'm going to play a song. One-by-one, I need everyone to come to the middle of the dance floor, dance with the Bride or the Groom for a few seconds, then get back to the circle." I would hold up a flash drive filled with music I made specifically for this event. I continued, "The most entertaining dance will win this flash drive of music I made especially for tonight!" The crowd gets excited! I hit the play button and "Stuck In The Middle With You" by Stealers Wheel starts to play. The music volume goes up, and when the beat hits, I hit the disco lights and the party is on its way! The excitement and energy that comes from the dancers is amazing! Get the others to clap their hands to the beat. The photographer and videographer get great shots! It's a win-win-win all the way around.

Sweet Sixteen Events. This technique also works perfectly with Sweet Sixteen or Quinceañera events. The process is the same, just change the song. Because these events are intended to celebrate an amazing young lady, you must choose a song that makes her feel extra special. Use the song, "Only Girl in The World" by Rihanna. To add some "musical drama"... show off your fancy lights at the bridge of the song. The crowd will love it.

Party Re-Starter

On occasion, you may need to play a slow song during your set. Most DJs hate this because it kills the dance floor and can completely destroy the vibe. Most DJs just ignore the request and keep playing. I never did. I looked at the situation as a challenge! Here's the best way I found to get the party back on track, typically at Weddings and corporate events. When the slow song is playing, your lights need to be turned down, of course. As the slow song ends, play "I'm Every Woman" by Whitney Houston. It starts out slow, so most people will think you're about to play another slow one. However, the dancers in the crowd know what's coming. Once the 1st beat hits, turn up a few lights. A few seconds later, the bassline hits. Turn the lights all the way up. Bam! Your dance floor gets full and you're back in control. Bonus: The ones that were slow dancing usually stay on the dance floor.

Keep It Festive

Another way to keep the vibe at a high level is to slightly "remind" the crowd why they are there. Throughout the evening, maybe once per hour, give the crowd a little jolt. I would also use this technique when I wanted to change from one genre of music to the next. If it's a Wedding, wait for a perfect time inside of a song (or transition) and say, "On the count of 3 say, 'Congratulations John & Mary! One… Two… Three!'" At the end of the night say, "On the count of three, say 'We love you John & Mary!'" If it's an anniversary, have the crowd say, "Congratulations on three". If it's a Prom, have the crowd say the name of the school. Etcetera, etcetera. It definitely helps to keep the vibe going at high levels, even for the people who are sitting in their chairs or who don't like to (nor want to) dance.

Mixing The Old With The New

One of the key elements of DJing a successful event is to play for everyone, not just the young, energetic dancers. A great way to appeal to both the older generation of dancers and the younger ones is to play original music, then play its "remixed" version. Many of the new songs today are being sampled (or are taking samples) from older music. I would suggest you play an original song, then mix in (or transition to) the newer, or updated version of the same song. The older crowd will immediately recognize the original song at first and the younger crowd will join in once you mix in the newer version of that same song. Hundreds of songs have been sampled over the years and have had tremendous success. You'd be surprised at the number of songs that did well in the U.S. markets, and also did well in markets overseas. (Imagine hearing your favorite song sampled in another language.) Try practicing with sampled songs and their sampled originals.

Here is a very small "sample" of music that has been sampled (multiple times) over the years:

- "Genius Of Love" by Tom Tom Club
- "Tom's Diner" by Suzanne Vega
- "Street Player" by Chicago
- "Got To Give It Up" by Marvin Gaye
- "I Like It" by DeBarge
- "Love Sensation" by Loleatta Holloway

Tip: Take a classic Rock n Roll song and remove the instruments, leaving only the lyrics. Next, take a hip hop banger of today and remove the lyrics. Now mash the 2 songs together. BAM! A good mashup of old school and new school always packs the dance floor.

Overtime

There will be times when the crowd is having a blast, but we all know that all good things must come to an end. The crowd will want the party to go on and on, but the people at the venue will be tired and will want you to stop playing. They want to go home. However, if you see that the crowd is fired up and wants to keep going, check with the event organizers to see if they would like to go into overtime. If so, confirm with the venue managers to ensure the extra time to keep playing. If you're able to keep the party going, make sure you get paid for your extra time! Usually, the organizers will pay cash. Consider this your overtime bonus. Get the cash and tuck it away before you keep the party going. It's a great feeling!

Give Thanks!

One last tip on how to separate your DJ business from your competition: Show appreciation by saying "Thank You". After every gig, look for the event organizers and thank them for the opportunity to play for them. Especially after Wedding events, look for the Bride, the Groom, and the Wedding planner. Thank them for giving you the opportunity to make their night as special as can be. Also find the venue manager to thank them for being great hosts because you may see them again in the future! If the venue managers see you often and become familiar with your brand, they just might give you free leads! The best venues only want to work with trustworthy vendors, so they will promote your business if you show respect and do a great job. Shake hands and give your business cards to the photographer and videographers because you may see them at future events, too. No matter the size or the nature of the gig, say "thank you" because it is a privilege to be able to do what you love and bring happiness and joy to so many people while doing it. Every gig is an opportunity to mold your life into something greater than you have ever imagined, so take advantage of every opportunity and be grateful for what has been given to you.

I wish you nothing but good times and great success with your DJ career!

Keep bangin' the beats!

NOTES

NOTES